AAT

Level 3

Diploma in Accounting

EPA Knowledge Assessment

Exam Practice Kit

For assessments from September 2024

BPP

First edition 2024

ISBN: 9781 0355 1806 7

British Library Cataloguing-in-Publication Data

A catalogue record for this book is available from the British Library

Published by

BPP Learning Media Ltd

BPP House, Aldine Place

142–144 Uxbridge Road

London W12 8AA

www.learningmedia.bpp.com

Printed in the United Kingdom

> Your learning materials, published by BPP Learning Media Ltd, are printed on paper obtained from traceable sustainable sources.

All rights reserved. No part of this publication may be reproduced, stored in a retrieval system or transmitted in any form or by any means, electronic, mechanical, photocopying, recording or otherwise, without the prior written permission of BPP Learning Media.

The contents of this course material are intended as a guide and not professional advice. Although every effort has been made to ensure that the contents of this course material are correct at the time of going to press, BPP Learning Media makes no warranty that the information in this course material is accurate or complete and accept no liability for any loss or damage suffered by any person acting or refraining from acting as a result of the material in this course material.

© BPP Learning Media Ltd

2024

A note about copyright

Dear Customer

What does the little © mean and why does it matter?

Your market-leading BPP books, course materials and e-learning materials do not write and update themselves. People write them on their own behalf or as employees of an organisation that invests in this activity. Copyright law protects their livelihoods. It does so by creating rights over the use of the content.

Breach of copyright is a form of theft – as well as being a criminal offence in some jurisdictions, it is potentially a serious breach of professional ethics.

With current technology, things might seem a bit hazy but, basically, without the express permission of BPP Learning Media:

- Photocopying our materials is a breach of copyright
- Printing our digital materials in order to share them with or forward them to a third party or use them in any way other than in connection with your BPP studies is a breach of copyright

NO AI TRAINING. Unless otherwise agreed in writing, the use of BPP material for the purpose of AI training is not permitted. Any use of this material to 'train' generative artificial intelligence (AI) technologies is prohibited, as is providing archived or cached data sets containing such material to another person or entity.

You can, of course, sell your books, in the form in which you have bought them – once you have finished with them. (Is this fair to your fellow students? We update for a reason.) Please note the e-products are sold on a single user licence basis: we do not supply 'unlock' codes to people who have bought them secondhand.

And what about outside the UK? BPP Learning Media strives to make our materials available at prices students can afford by local printing arrangements, pricing policies and partnerships which are clearly listed on our website. A tiny minority ignore this and indulge in criminal activity by illegally photocopying our material or supporting organisations that do. If they act illegally and unethically in one area, can you really trust them?

Contents

Introduction — iv

Question and answer index	Questions	Answers
Chapter 1 – Tax Processes for Business (TPFB)	8	79
Chapter 2 – Financial Accounting: Preparing Financial Statements (FAPS)	40	93
Chapter 3 – Management Accounting Techniques (MATS)	56	101
Chapter 4 – Business Awareness (BUAW)	67	110
AAT Practice Assessment	123	
BPP Practice Assessment 1	127	141
BPP Practice Assessment 2	151	165
BPP Practice Assessment 3	175	189

Review form

Introduction

This is BPP Learning Media's AAT Exam Practice Kit for the *Level 3 EPA Knowledge Assessment*. It is part of a suite of ground-breaking resources produced by BPP Learning Media for AAT assessments.

This Exam Practice Kit has been carefully designed to enable students to practise all of the learning outcomes and assessment criteria for the units that make up *Diploma in Accounting Level 3 EPA Knowledge Assessment*. It is fully up to date as at July 2024 and reflects both the AAT's qualification specification and the practice assessments provided by the AAT.

This Exam Practice Kit contains these key features:

- Tasks corresponding to each assessment objective in the specification. Some tasks in the Exam Practice Kit are designed for learning purposes, others are of assessment standard.
- In the main Exam Practice Kit there may occasionally be links to online information (such as AAT Ethics). These are there to assist you in the practice of these questions. In the real assessment you will be supplied with a number of appendices which may include extracts of the AAT *Code of Professional Ethics* and/or VAT information.
- Further BPP practice assessments.

The emphasis in all tasks and assessments is on the practical application of the skills acquired.

Assessment method: Knowledge assessment

The knowledge assessment will be administered in a controlled and invigilated environment. Apprentices are given the opportunity to demonstrate their application of knowledge gained to specific scenarios. The scenarios will focus on application of logic and reason to resolve real-world scenarios typically encountered in an apprentices on-programme training. The pass mark for the assessment is 70%.

Assessment method	Marking type	Duration of assessment	Marks
Computer-based assessment	Results will be available within 24 hours from submitting the assessment. **Note**: For initial assessments, results will be available within 10 days of submitting the assessment. This timeframe will be reviewed once a statistically reliable volume of students have completed the assessment	2 hours and 30 minutes (90 minutes for the assessment and a further 60 minutes for reflection and planning as needed).	40

Assessment objectives

Assessment objective	Contribution to overall grade
AO1 – Financial statements and bookkeeping (K1, K2, K3, K5, S2, S3, S4, S5)	50%
AO2 – Professional standards (S4, S6)	12.5%
AO3 – Digital and data security (K6, K8)	12.5%
AO4 – Financial investigation and queries (K4, S1, S6)	25%
	100%

Administration

The assessment is open book which means that the apprentice can refer to reference books or materials used during their course of study for the apprenticeship whilst completing the tasks.

The following equipment is allowed to be used during the assessment:
- pens, pencils erasers; and
- a scientific or accountancy calculator. Calculators must not emit audible tones or function as any other digital device.

Apprentices must **not** have access to the internet for the duration of the assessment. This includes any potential technological, web-enabled sources of information such as, but not limited to, iPods, mobile phones, MP3/4 players, smart watches which have a data storage device.

No other equipment is allowed.

The knowledge assessment **must** be taken in the presence of an invigilator.

Approaching the assessment

When you sit the assessment, it is very important that you follow the on-screen instructions. This means you need to carefully read the instructions, both on the introduction screens and during specific tasks.

When you access the assessment, you should be presented with an introductory screen with information similar to that shown below.

> You have **2 hours and 30 minutes** to complete this practice assessment.
> - This assessment contains **3 tasks** and you should attempt to complete every task.
> - Each task is independent. You will not need to refer to your answers to previous tasks.
> - The total number of marks for this assessment is **40**.
> - Read every task carefully to make sure you understand what is required.
> - Where the date is relevant, it is given in the task data.
> - Both minus signs and brackets can be used to indicate negative numbers unless task instructions state otherwise.
> - You must use a full stop to indicate a decimal point. For example, write 100.57 not 100,57 or 10057.
> - You may use a comma to indicate a number in the thousands, but you don't have to. For example, 10000 and 10,000 are both acceptable.
>
> Scenario
>
> Tasks 1 to 3 are based on the workplace scenario of Company X, which manufactures vehicles.
>
> **Once you have clicked 'Continue' you will not be able to return to this page. You will be able to view the 'Assessment information' in the references section at each task position.**

It is very important you read the instructions on the introductory screen and apply them in the assessment. You don't want to lose marks when you know the correct answer just because you have not entered it in the right format.

In general, the rules set out in the AAT practice assessments for the subject you are studying for will apply in the real assessment, but you should carefully read the information on this screen again in the real assessment, just to make sure. This screen may also confirm the VAT rate used if applicable.

A full stop is needed to indicate a decimal point. We would recommend using minus signs to indicate negative numbers and leaving out the comma signs to indicate thousands, as this results in a lower number of key strokes and less margin for error when working under time pressure. Having said that, you can use whatever is easiest for you as long as you operate within the rules set out for your particular assessment.

You have to show competence throughout the assessment and you should therefore complete all of the tasks. Don't leave questions unanswered.

In some assessments, written or complex tasks may be human marked. In this case you are given a blank space or table to enter your answer into. You are told in the assessments which tasks these are. Note there may be none if all answers are marked by the computer.

If these involve calculations, it is a good idea to decide in advance how you are going to lay out your answers to such tasks by practising answering them on a word document, and certainly you should try all such tasks in this Exam Practice Kit and in the AAT's Lifelong Learning platform using the practice assessment.

When asked to fill in tables, or gaps, never leave any blank even if you are unsure of the answer. Fill in your best estimate.

Note that for some assessments where there is a lot of scenario information or tables of data provided (eg tax tables), you may need to access these via 'pop-ups'. Instructions will be provided on how you can bring up the necessary data during the assessment.

Finally, take note of any task specific instructions once you are in the assessment. For example, you may be asked to enter a date in a certain format or to enter a number to a certain number of decimal places.

Retakes

An apprentice who fails can re-take at their employer's discretion.

An apprentice should have a supportive action plan to prepare for a re-take.

The timescale for a re-take is dependent on how much re-training is required and is typically taken within 3 months of the EPA outcome notification.

Failed assessment methods must be re-taken within a 6-month period from the EPA outcome notification, otherwise the entire EPA will need to be re-taken in full.

Re-takes are not offered to an apprentice wishing to move from pass to a higher grade.

Supplements

From time to time, we may need to publish supplementary materials to one of our titles. This can be for a variety of reasons. From a small change in the AAT unit guidance to new legislation coming into effect between editions.

You should check our supplements page regularly for anything that may affect your learning materials. All supplements are available free of charge on our supplements page on our website at: learningmedia.bpp.com/pages/resources-for-students

Improving material and removing errors

BPP Learning Media do everything possible to ensure the material is accurate and up to date when sending to print. In the event that any errors are found after the print date, they are uploaded to the following website: learningmedia.bpp.com/pages/errata

Questions

Chapter 1 – Tax Processes for Business (TPFB)

TPFB Summaries

The diagrams that follow are summaries from 'Tax Processes for Business (TPFB)' covering the key areas most relevant to your EPA Knowledge assessment. The summaries and tasks included in this chapter are based on the AAT 'Scope of content – knowledge assessment' mapping contained in the AAT End Point Assessment Specification.

Introduction to VAT

Introduction to VAT

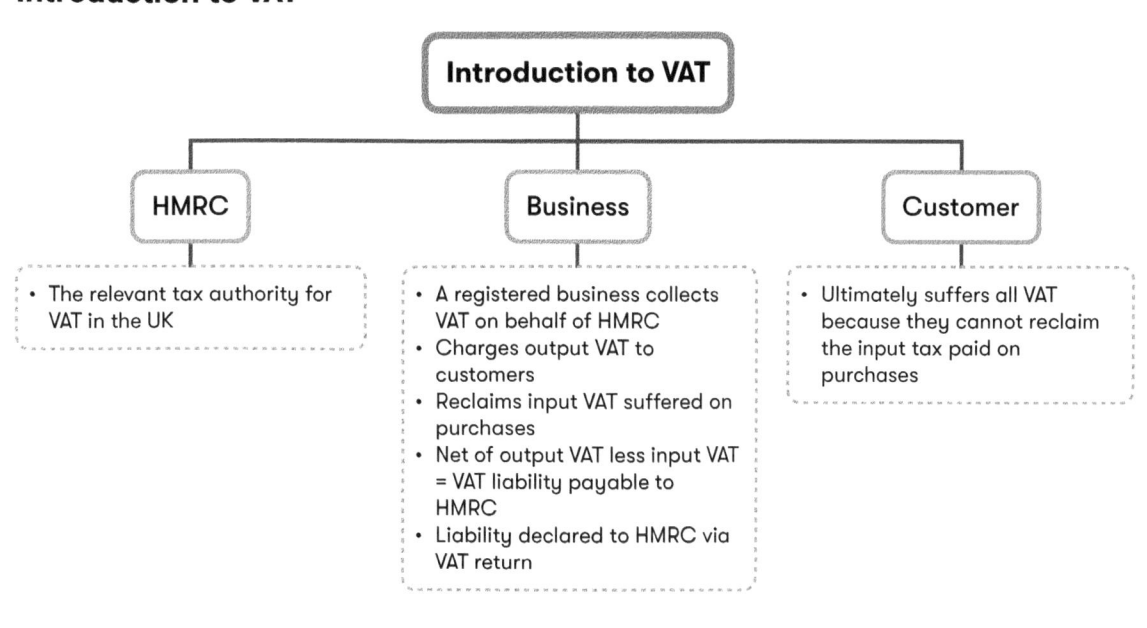

HMRC
- The relevant tax authority for VAT in the UK

Business
- A registered business collects VAT on behalf of HMRC
- Charges output VAT to customers
- Reclaims input VAT suffered on purchases
- Net of output VAT less input VAT = VAT liability payable to HMRC
- Liability declared to HMRC via VAT return

Customer
- Ultimately suffers all VAT because they cannot reclaim the input tax paid on purchases

VAT basics

VAT basics

Scope of VAT

Taxable supplies
- Taxable supplies are at standard rate (20%), reduced rate (5%) or zero rated (0%)
- Taxable persons making taxable supplies can recover input VAT on business purchases

Exempt supplies
- Exempt suppliers not permitted to register for VAT
- No VAT on sales
- Exempt traders cannot recover any input VAT (all costs gross in accounts)

Registration

Compulsory
- Past (historic) turnover exceeds registration threshold in previous 12 months (cumulative)
- Future turnover will exceed registration threshold in next 30 days alone
- Deregistration compulsory if cease to make taxable supplies, voluntary if taxable supplies fall under deregistration threshold

Voluntary
- Advantages: recover input VAT, avoid penalties for late registration, business looks more substantial
- Disadvantages: obligation to file VAT returns, keep records, issue VAT invoices, exposure to penalties for errors and late filing, prices increase if customers cannot reclaim VAT

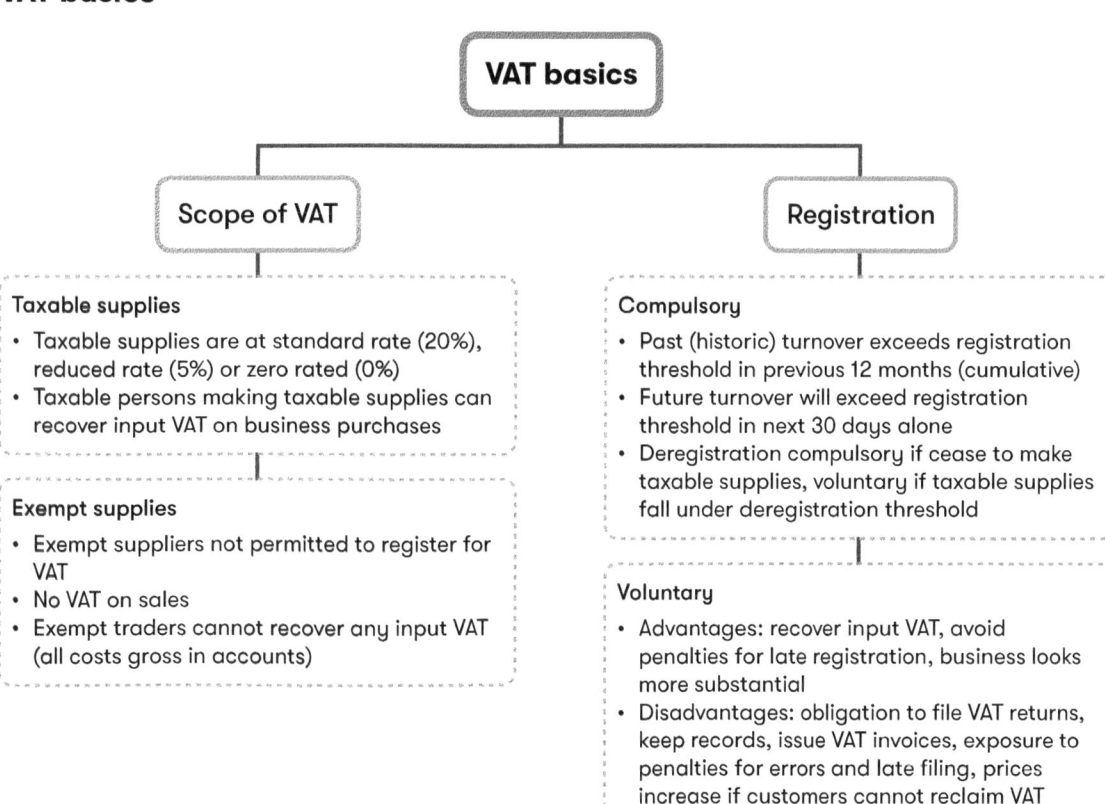

Inputs and outputs

Inputs and Outputs

Calculation of VAT
- Price given inclusive of VAT:
  - × 20/120 if standard-rated
  - × 5/105 if reduced-rated
- Price given exclusive of VAT: × 20% or 5% to get VAT
- VAT usually rounded down to nearest 1p
- VAT liability = output VAT – recoverable input VAT for the period

Irrecoverable input VAT
- Cannot recover input VAT on:
  - UK Business entertaining
  - Cars
  - Private use items
- VAT on private fuel is recoverable but add fuel scale charge to output VAT

Partially exempt traders
- Make taxable and exempt supplies (only charge VAT on taxable supplies)
- Must attribute or apportion input VAT between taxable and exempt supplies
- Input VAT re exempt supplies is recoverable if meet de minimis test

Overseas transactions
- Imports – pay input VAT at border or via postponed accounting. Recover as per usual rules
- Exports – always zero rated if proof of export
- Service supplied overseas – charge UK VAT if BTC
- Service purchased from overseas – reverse charge input VAT as for postponed accounting

The VAT return

The VAT return

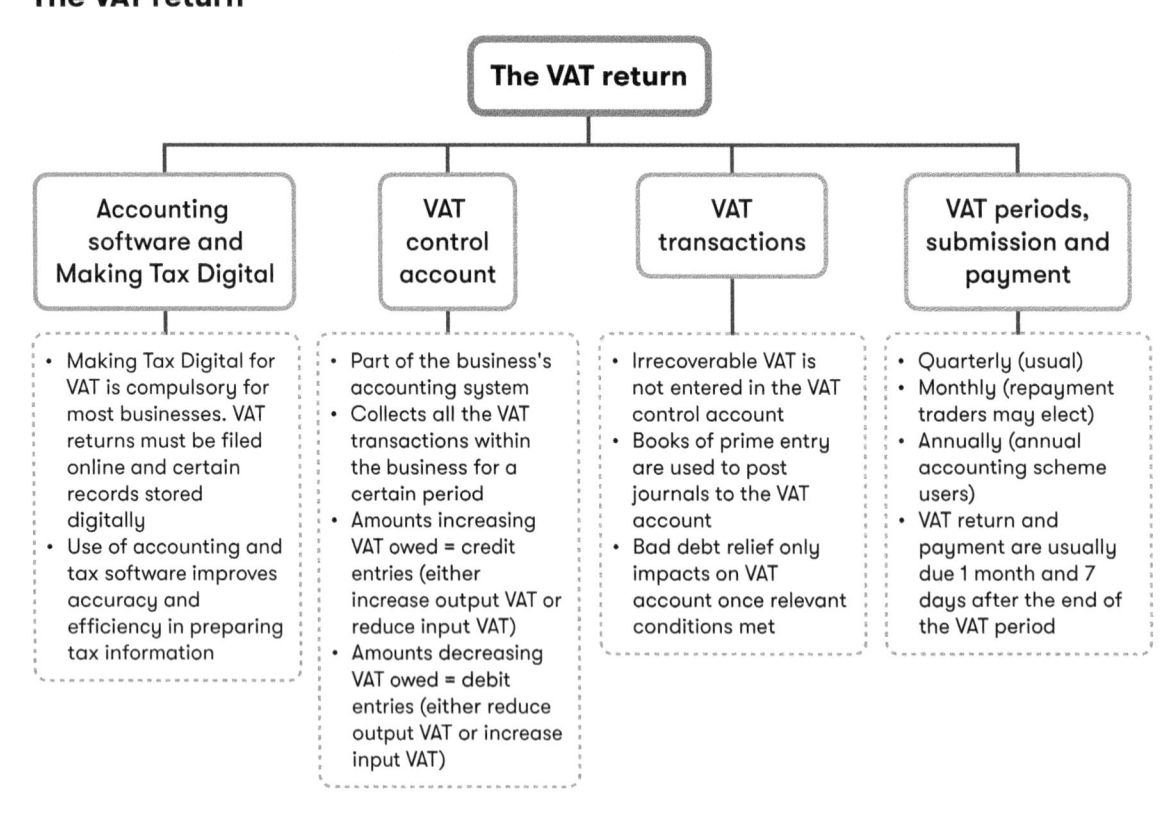

Accounting software and Making Tax Digital
- Making Tax Digital for VAT is compulsory for most businesses. VAT returns must be filed online and certain records stored digitally
- Use of accounting and tax software improves accuracy and efficiency in preparing tax information

VAT control account
- Part of the business's accounting system
- Collects all the VAT transactions within the business for a certain period
- Amounts increasing VAT owed = credit entries (either increase output VAT or reduce input VAT)
- Amounts decreasing VAT owed = debit entries (either reduce output VAT or increase input VAT)

VAT transactions
- Irrecoverable VAT is not entered in the VAT control account
- Books of prime entry are used to post journals to the VAT account
- Bad debt relief only impacts on VAT account once relevant conditions met

VAT periods, submission and payment
- Quarterly (usual)
- Monthly (repayment traders may elect)
- Annually (annual accounting scheme users)
- VAT return and payment are usually due 1 month and 7 days after the end of the VAT period

Accounting for VAT

Accounting for VAT

VAT records and invoices

- Accounting records are used to record VAT transactions and verify VAT returns. Certain records must be held digitally, eg all VAT charged and paid, the time and value of sales and purchases
- VAT invoices have certain required content to be valid. Without a valid invoice, input VAT cannot be reclaimed (except on certain items costing less than £25)
- Different types of VAT invoice:
  - Simplified VAT invoices – may be issued for supplies <£250
  - Modified invoice required for retail sales >£250, must show total VAT-inclusive cost
  - Electronic VAT invoices are permitted but with stringent HMRC conditions
- VAT invoices where customer will reverse charge the VAT, eg under CIS, must make clear that reverse charge applies and state the amount or rate of VAT to be charged

Discounts, credit and debit notes

- VAT always applies on amount net of discounts Supplier has two options re settlement discounts:
  - Invoice full amount then credit note if discount taken
  - Issue invoice with two possible VAT amounts (on price before and after discount)
- VAT invoices cannot be amended after issue
- Credit notes must be issued to correct over-charged VAT
- These reduce output tax for the supplier and input tax for the customer

Timing

- Tax point = usually earliest of supply (basic tax point) invoice or cash. 14 day invoice rule can override BTP
- Tax point = date used to account for VAT
- Bad debt relief can only apply where invoice more than 6 months overdue. Supplier reclaims VAT by increasing input tax

VAT schemes for small businesses

VAT schemes for small businesses

Standard scheme
- Default scheme
- VAT return every quarter
- 1m 7 days to submit and pay

Cash accounting scheme
- Frequency as for standard scheme
- Eligible if turnover <£1.35m p.a
- VAT paid and recovered on cash basis (ie ignore normal tax point rules)
- Good for traders offering long credit terms to customers
- Can combine with annual accounting

Annual accounting scheme
- Annual return, due within 2 months of year end
- Eligible if turnover <£1.35m p.a
- Nine interim payments of 10% of prior year liability, or 3 interim payments of 25%
- Annual liability less POAs = due with return
- Reduced admin and smoother VAT cash flows
- Can combine with other schemes

Flat rate scheme
- VAT liability is an industry-specific % × gross total turnover (including exempt supplies)
- Eligible if taxable turnover <£150,000 pa
- Can only recover input VAT on fixed assets costing >£2,000
- Easy VAT calculation
- Can combine with annual accounting

Payroll systems

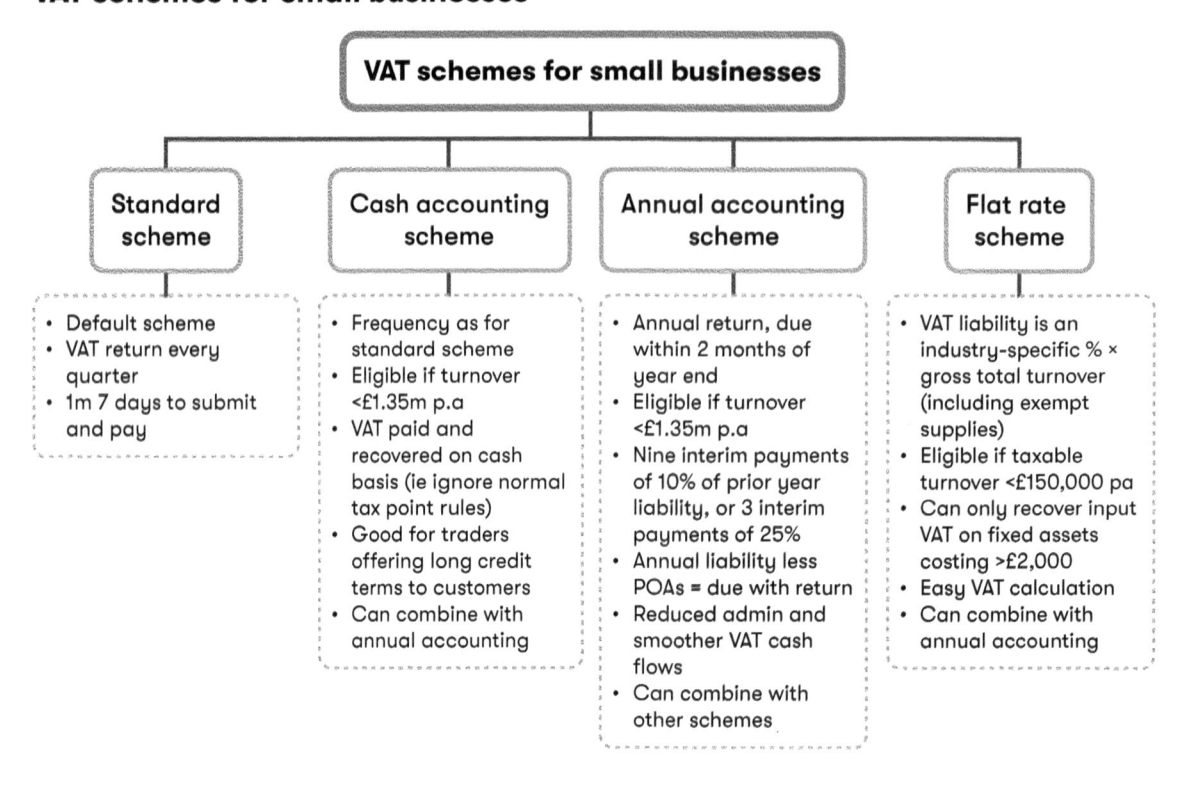

Payroll systems

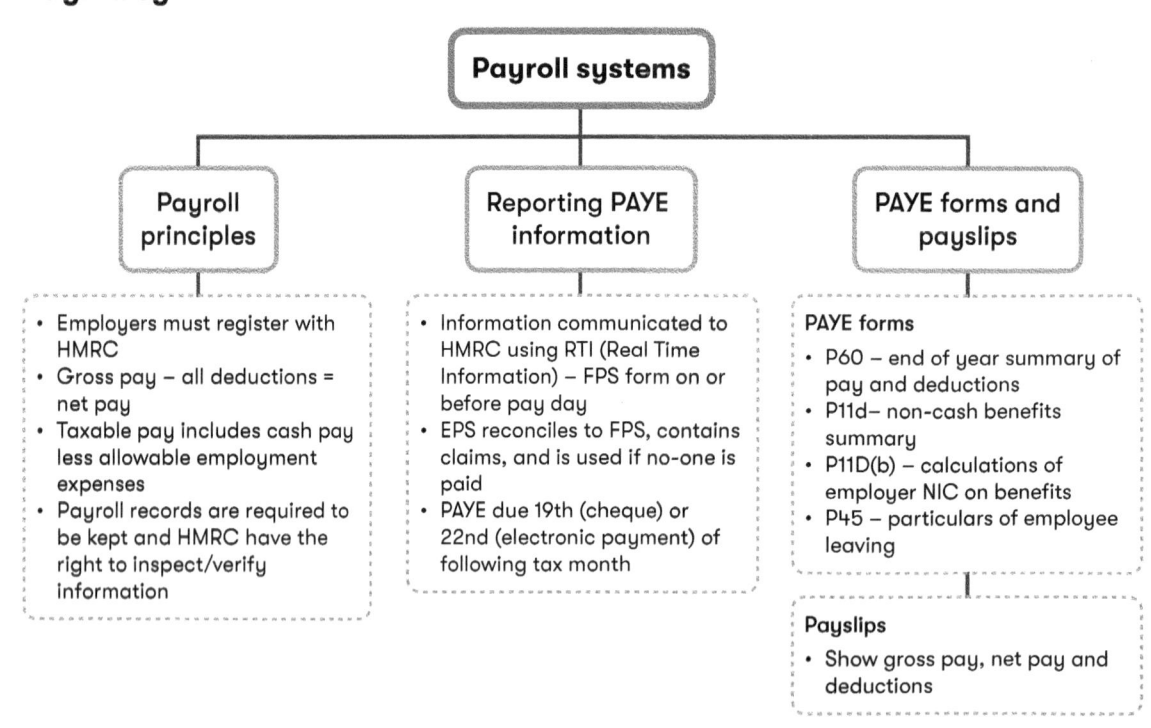

Payroll principles
- Employers must register with HMRC
- Gross pay – all deductions = net pay
- Taxable pay includes cash pay less allowable employment expenses
- Payroll records are required to be kept and HMRC have the right to inspect/verify information

Reporting PAYE information
- Information communicated to HMRC using RTI (Real Time Information) – FPS form on or before pay day
- EPS reconciles to FPS, contains claims, and is used if no-one is paid
- PAYE due 19th (cheque) or 22nd (electronic payment) of following tax month

PAYE forms and payslips

PAYE forms
- P60 – end of year summary of pay and deductions
- P11d – non-cash benefits summary
- P11D(b) – calculations of employer NIC on benefits
- P45 – particulars of employee leaving

Payslips
- Show gross pay, net pay and deductions

VAT and PAYE Administration

VAT and PAYE Administration

VAT errors
- Small errors (less than error correction threshold) adjusted on next VAT return
- Error correction threshold is higher of £10,000 or 1% of turnover (max £50k)
- Larger errors or deliberate underpayment separately reported on Form VAT652

Penalties

VAT penalties apply to:
- Errors (0-100% × underpaid VAT)
- Late returns/payment – Default Surcharge Scheme applies, and penalties apply to subsequent late payments
- Failure to register – % of VAT due
- Record keeping – £3,000 per accounting period

PAYE penalties
- Errors – penalties as per VAT errors
- FP /EPS late – £100-£400 penalty
- Late monthly PAYE payment more than once in a tax year – penalties apply to 2nd and subsequent late payments
- Late payment of other amounts – 5-15% penalty
- Record keeping – as per VAT

Communications

Clients should be informed of:
- Change in tax rates and impact on their business/customers
- Impact of registration on profitability and compliance obligations
- Taxes payable and deadlines, to avoid penalties

Contact with HMRC:
- Advice: check website, helpline, then contact HMRC directly
- Maintain up-to-date knowledge via websites/journals
- Control visits: HMRC must give prior notice and are entitled to question the owner, inspect records and watch the business

Ethics
- Tax advisers must adhere to ethical principles when giving tax advice

TPFB Practice Tasks

Task 1.1

The following tasks are based on the workplace scenario of Notes To Go.

You are Arvo, a part-qualified accounting technician. You have recently begun to work for Notes To Go, a VAT-registered business which sells printed music.

Notes To Go is run by Max and Judith in partnership. You handle the bookkeeping and VAT compliance under Judith's supervision

Required

(a) Notes To Go wishes to reclaim VAT on its purchases. Are these statements true or false?

	True ✓	False ✓
Notes To Go may reclaim VAT on its purchases through its VAT returns.		
The VAT on Notes To Go's purchases is known as output tax.		

Notes To Go has purchased two items:

Standard-rated stationery for total £120

Exempt postage stamps for total £120

Required

(b) What is the net cost of these to Notes To Go?

	✓
Stationary net cost £100	
Stationary net cost £120	
Postage stamps net cost £120	
Postage stamps net cost £100	

The printed music Notes To Go sells is zero-rated.

Required

(c) Which of the following statements is/are true?

	True ✓	False ✓
Notes To Go is making exempt supplies.		
The amount of VAT on any sale of printed music will be zero.		

(d) Select which of the following are advantages of Notes To Go being registered for VAT.

	✓
Registration may improve the image of the business.	
VAT returns need to be prepared on a regular basis.	
VAT on Notes To Go's purchases may be reclaimed.	

Total sales income received by Notes To Go last year was £110,000.

Required

(e) Complete the following sentences using the picklists below.

Turnover last year was ▢ ▼ the VAT registration threshold.

Notes To Go could apply to HMRC to deregister ▢ ▼ .

If Notes To Go deregistered, issuing VAT receipts in the future would be ▢ ▼ .

Picklist
- Above
- Because supplies are zero-rated
- Below
- If turnover is low enough
- Optional
- Prohibited

You notice that your employer's electricity bill includes standard-rated VAT, but your own home electricity bill includes VAT at the reduced rate. Both bills are for £210 inclusive of VAT.

Required

(f) Complete the following sentences using the picklist below.

Your employer's electricity bill is ▢ ▼ net of VAT.

Your home electricity bill is ▢ ▼ net of VAT.

The VAT on your home electricity bill is borne by ▢ ▼ .

Picklist
- HMRC
- Yourself
- £168
- £175
- £200
- £210

Task 1.2

The following tasks are based on the following workplace scenario of Harpreet.

You are Charlie, a part-qualified accounting technician. You work for an accountancy practice whose clients include Harpreet. Harpreet runs a local sweet shop.

Harpreet has employed a new junior staff member, Wei. You are explaining some basic concepts of VAT to Wei.

Required

(a) Complete the following sentences using the picklists below.

VAT is initially collected by [▼] .

VAT is eventually borne by [▼] .

Picklist
- HMRC
- The final consumer
- Traders

(b) Complete the following sentences using the picklists below.

VAT is an indirect tax because it is based on [▼] .

The sweets sold by Harpreet are [▼] .

Picklist
- Business profits
- Goods
- Services
- Transactions

(c) Which of the following statements is/are true or false?

	True ✓	False ✓
We only need to charge VAT if our customers are also VAT registered.		
We do not need to charge VAT if our customers pay in cash.		

(d) Select which of the following statements are correct about the 'VAT fraction'.

	✓
The VAT fraction can be used to find the VAT from the gross sales price.	
The VAT fraction for reduced-rated supplies is 5%.	

The shop has purchased standard-rated sweets for £180.

Required

(e) Calculate the net cost of these sweets to the shop.

Sweets: £ [   ]

The shop has purchased zero-rated children's colouring books for £180.

Required

(f) Calculate the net cost of the books to the shop.

Children's colouring books £ [   ]

(g) Complete the following sentences using the picklists below.

VAT returns are usually made for [▼].

The deadline for submission is [▼] and [▼] after the three-month VAT return period.

The deadline for BACS or CHAPS payment is [▼].

VAT direct debits are taken [▼] [▼] after the normal payment deadline.

Picklist
- Days
- One month
- One month later
- Seven
- Seven days
- The same as for the return
- Three
- Three months
- Working days

Task 1.3

The following tasks are based around the transactions of a company called Camden Ltd.

You are Sansa, a part-qualified accounting technician. You work for an accountancy practice whose clients include Camden Ltd.

Camden Ltd makes both taxable and exempt supplies. The company also purchases some business items from a supplier in the USA, and sells goods to customers in Japan.

The following information is available for Camden Ltd's VAT quarter to 31 December:

	£
Input VAT	
Relating to taxable supplies	5,000
Relating to exempt supplies	1,100
Unallocated	3,000
Total	9,100
Supplies	
Taxable supplies total	25,000
Exempt supplies total	3,200

Required

(a) Allocate the total input VAT of £9,100 between taxable and exempt supplies using the tables below.

Attributable to taxable supplies

	£
Directly allocated	
Indirectly allocated:	
Total taxable inputs	

Attributable to exempt supplies

	£
Directly allocated	
Indirectly allocated:	
Total exempt inputs	

(b) Complete the following sentences.

The total of the exempt input VAT is only recoverable if it is [▼] the [▼] limit:

The amount is below [▼] per month on average, [▼] it is ≤ [▼] of the total input tax for the period.

Picklist
- 20%
- 50%
- Above
- And
- Below
- De minimis
- Minimal
- Or
- £625
- £650

Use your answers from the above questions to complete this requirement.

Required

(c) How much of Camden Ltd's total input VAT of £9,100 can be reclaimed?

Input VAT to recover is £ [   ]

Camden Ltd is selling some standard rated goods to a business in Japan.

Required

(d) **Which of the following statements are true?**

	✓
Output VAT of 20% will be charged on the sale, and this can be recovered as input VAT on the next VAT return.	
Goods sold to overseas customers are referred to as exports.	
Exports are always zero rated, provided the trader obtains evidence of their export within three months.	
Exports are always exempt, provided the trader obtains evidence of their export within three months.	

Camden Ltd is purchasing some goods from a business in the USA.

Required

(e) **Complete the following sentences using the picklists below.**

Goods which are purchased from overseas countries are known as [▼].

[▼] is charged by the supplier. When the goods enter the UK, the

[▼] needs to pay the applicable rate of UK VAT.

Picklist
- 20%
- Exports
- Imports
- No VAT
- Purchaser
- Seller
- VAT

Task 1.4

The following tasks are based on the workplace scenario of TaxTix LLP.

You are Britt, a part-qualified accounting technician. You are employed by tax accountants, TaxTix LLP, where you assist with bookkeeping and VAT compliance for various business clients of the firm.

A client has phoned TaxTix LLP to ask for advice on whether they need purchase invoices for two items for VAT purposes.

Required

(a) **Select which of the following invoices they must keep.**

	✓
£20 spent at a toll bridge while travelling.	
Goods costing £35 bought from a vending machine.	

(b) Complete the following sentences using the picklists below.

All records [▼] be kept digitally, and certain records [▼] be kept digitally under 'Making Tax Digital' rules.

All records are to be kept for at least [▼] years.

Picklist
- May
- Must
- Seven
- Six
- Three

Henrik, a new trainee, shows you two purchase invoices addressed to TaxTix LLP. No VAT is shown on these invoices and Henrik asks you what the amount of VAT is for each invoice.

Required

(c) Calculate the amount of VAT on standard-rated consultancy services with a total price of £398.00.

Amount of VAT £ [   ]

Following on from the above requirement.

Required

(d) Calculate the amount of VAT on Zero-rated food costing £120.00

Amount of VAT £ [   ]

TaxTix LLP has a few clients who are very late payers. Your manager has asked you to investigate when VAT bad debt relief may be claimed.

Required

(e) Which of the following is a condition for claiming bad debt relief?

	✓
The debt must be more than six years overdue.	
The input tax must have been paid by the client.	
The output tax must have been paid to HMRC.	

(f) Is this statement true or false regarding VAT bad debt relief?

	True ✓	False ✓
Relief is claimed through the VAT return as a deduction from output tax.		

Henrik has been asked to make the accounting entries to write off a bad debt. This was a fee of £1,000 plus £200 VAT billed to a former client. Henrik is not sure which accounts to debit and credit and asks you to assist.

Required

(g) **Complete the following sentences using the picklists below.**

Bad debts expense account is [____▼____] with [____▼____].

The VAT account is [____▼____] with [____▼____].

The sales ledger control account is [____▼____] with [____▼____].

Picklist
- Credited
- Debited
- £1,000
- £1,200
- £200

Task 1.5

The following tasks are based on the workplace of D's Doors.

You are Daisuke, a part-qualified accounting technician. You work for D's Doors, a sole trader business run by Debbie. The business sells and fits doors, and is registered for VAT.

All the supplies D's Doors makes are of standard-rated. Most of the customers of the business are individual householders but there are also some business clients.

Debbie would like to offer discounts to some of the customers of D's Doors.

Required

(a) **Complete the following sentence using the picklist below.**

Debbie would like to offer a 5% discount to Bizyness Ltd if they buy 20 or more doors in a single order.

If Bizyness Ltd goes ahead and orders 20 doors at one time, the discount would be a

[____▼____] discount.

Picklist
- Prompt payment
- Trade

(b) **Complete the following sentence using the picklists below.**

Debbie would like to offer a 5% discount to Harold if he buys a back door and pays within 14 days of this being fitted.

The discount offered would be a [____▼____] or [____▼____] discount.

Picklist
- Bulk
- Prompt payment
- Settlement
- Trade

Harold has ordered the back door. He is not certain yet whether he will pay within 14 days of his door being fitted. Debbie would like to issue a single invoice so that no credit note is needed for early payment.

Required

(c) Which of the following must the invoice show?

	✓
The deadline for payment for the discount to apply.	
The amount of the discount.	
The VAT on the discounted price.	
A statement that no credit note will be issued.	

Debbie receives an order for 3 new doors on 1 April 20X8. She sends out the order on 13 April 20X8 and issues the invoice on 20 April 20X8.

Required

(d) Complete the following sentence using the picklist below.

The actual tax point is [▼].

Picklist
- 1 April 20X8
- 13 April 20X8
- 20 April 20X8

Erna ordered a new security door on 31 December 20X8. She paid a deposit of £500 on 16 January 20X9. On 30 January, her new door was dispatched. Debbie (D Doors) issued an invoice to Erna on 18 February 20X9 for the full invoiced amount of £1200 showing the outstanding balance to be paid of £700. Erna paid the outstanding amount on 23 February 20X9.

Required

(e) Complete the following sentences.

The tax point for the deposit of £500 is [▼].

The tax point for the balance of £700 is [▼].

Picklist
- 16 January 20X9
- 18 February 20X9
- 23 February 20X9
- 30 January 20X9
- 31 December 20X8

Task 1.6

Debbie, who runs D Doors sole trader business, has asked for some illustrations of how discounts and credit notes will affect her business figures. She would also like some general information on accounting records.

For the standard-rated sale, use the same value before VAT and fill in the amounts you are asked for.

D's Doors

Standard-rated doors offered to a customer for the value of £2,400.00.

Discount of 10% offered for payment within 7 days.

Discount of 5% offered for payment within 14 days.

Required

(a) Using the proforma layout provided, fill in all the unshaded boxes.

	Paid in 7 days time £	Paid in 14 days time £	Paid in 20 days time £
Net value	2,400	2,400	2,400
Discount %			
Discounted net value			
VAT on standard rated goods			
Gross amount payable by the customer			

Debbie has sent a credit note to a customer.

Required

(b) As a result of issuing this credit note, will Debbie have to pay more, or less VAT to HMRC?

	✓
More VAT payable	
Less VAT payable	

Debbie sells two doors to a customer for £1,000 plus VAT but allows a settlement discount of 5% for payment within ten days.

The customer pays after eight days. Debbie decided to invoice for the full amount only.

Required

(c) What is the correct action for Debbie?

	✓
Issue a credit note for £50 including VAT	
Take no action	
Issue a further invoice for £50 plus VAT	
Issue a credit note for £50 plus VAT	

If Debbie offers a settlement discount, the VAT charged must be based on the actual consideration received. There are two ways of achieving this.

Required

(d) Complete the following sentences using the picklists below.

Debbie can issue an invoice for the [▼], followed by a [▼] if the discount [▼].

or

Debbie can issue [▼], with [▼] possible prices and VAT amounts specified, with clear instructions to the customer regarding recoverability of their input VAT.

Picklist
- Both
- Credit note
- Debit note
- Different
- Full amount
- Is not taken up
- Is taken up
- Net amount
- One invoice
- Two invoices

Debbie is making both cash and credit sales.

Required

(e) In order to calculate the correct amount of output tax for Debbie's business, which of the following accounting records will be needed?

	✓
Sales daybook	
Purchases daybook	
Cash receipts book	
Cash payments book	

Task 1.7

The following tasks are based on the workplace scenario of Kaykes.

You are Kim, a part-qualified accounting technician. You and your brother Kevin, a professional cook, are setting up a cookery business in your spare time near your home in London. You handle the bookkeeping and VAT compliance.

A possible new client has contacted Kaykes. This is a large business called Sate Ltd. Sate Ltd's financial controller asks Kevin whether you can provide full VAT invoices if they buy large numbers of cakes on repeat order.

Kevin says yes and is now asking you what needs to go onto a full VAT invoice.

Required

(a) Which of the following are elements of a full VAT invoice?

	✓
A sequential invoice number	
The time of the supply	
Details of the deadline for payment	
The date of issue of the document (where different to the time of supply)	
Kaykes' address	
Kaykes' VAT registration number as supplier	
The date from which Kaykes was registered for VAT	
A brief description of the type(s) of cake	
The number of each type of cake bought	
Sate Ltd's address	
Sate Ltd's Company registration number	
Sate Ltd's VAT registration number	
A £ sign to show the currency	
The rate of VAT	
The total amount of VAT chargeable	

Kevin has asked you for some general information around VAT invoices.

Required

(b) Which TWO of the following statements about VAT invoices are correct?

	✓
VAT-registered businesses must raise a VAT invoice (paper or electronic) when they make a taxable supply to another VAT-registered business.	
A taxable person can always reclaim input VAT.	
If the customer is not VAT-registered, a VAT invoice is still mandatory.	
A VAT invoice must be raised within 30 days of the supply.	

Kevin is considering issuing electronic invoices and he asks you if there are conditions required to issue invoices electronically.

Required

(c) Which TWO of the following are required for HMRC to permit invoices to be issued electronically?

	✓
Kaykes will need to implement procedures to ensure the authenticity and integrity of their electronic invoices.	
Kaykes' customers must settle the invoices via bank transfer.	
Kaykes' customers must agree to receive electronic invoices.	
The file type must enable invoices to be amended (eg Word document).	
HMRC must receive copies of all electronic invoices issued.	

Kevin has heard about simplified and modified invoices, he asks you for some details around these two types of invoices.

Required

(d) Complete the following sentences using the picklists below.

For supplies invoiced at [▼] than £250, including VAT, a business may issue a less detailed [▼] invoice.

If [▼] are sold for [▼] than £250, a [▼] invoice may be issued.

Picklist
- Any supplies
- Less
- Modified
- More
- Retail supplies
- Simplified

VAT schemes for small businesses

Task 1.8

The following tasks are based on the workplace scenario of Mo.

You are Mo, a part-qualified accounting technician employed by EeZee plc, which produces and sells electronic equipment.

EeZee plc has made the following sales and purchases in the current VAT quarter:

- Standard-rated sales £20,000
- Exempt sales £9,000
- Standard-rated purchases of components £4,000
- Standard-rated services purchased £1,400
- Donation to charity £100
- Applicable flat rate 7.5%

Required

(a) Calculate the amount of VAT due for the current quarter.

The amount of VAT due is £ ☐

(b) Complete the following sentences using the picklists below.

The VAT payable to HMRC calculated above is shown in ☐ of the VAT return.

The figure shown in box 6 will be ☐ which is the total VAT- ☐ sales.

Picklist
- Box 1
- Box 3
- Box 6
- Exclusive
- Inclusive
- Standard rated
- £2,475
- £24,000
- £33,000

(c) Complete the following sentence using the picklists below.

A business can apply to register for the flat rate scheme provided that [▼] taxable turnover is not expected to exceed [▼] in the next [▼] months.

Picklist
- 12
- 24
- 3
- Exclusive
- Inclusive
- VAT-exclusive
- VAT-inclusive
- £100,000
- £150,000
- £230,000

(d) Which of the following statements are true about the flat rate scheme?

	✓
Output VAT is not paid until it has been collected from the customer, giving a cash flow advantage.	
Cashflow can be managed as the VAT is payable based on a percentage of turnover.	
Only one VAT return needs to be submitted.	
VAT payable is normally less than the amount payable under the standard accounting scheme.	
A business can choose which flat rate percentage it wants to use in order to calculate the lowest VAT liability.	
There will be simplified administration as VAT does not have to be accounted for on each individual sales or purchase invoice.	
A business using the flat rate scheme can always claim back input VAT on larger fixed assets.	

EeZee plc has asked you for some information about the cash accounting scheme.

Required

(e) Show which of the following statements about the cash accounting scheme are true or false.

	True ✓	False ✓
Businesses using the flat rate scheme can also use the cash accounting scheme.		
The scheme can only be used when a business's VAT-exclusive taxable turnover is not expected to exceed £1,350,000 in the next 12 months.		

	True ✓	False ✓
A business must leave the cash accounting scheme if VAT-exclusive taxable supplies exceed £1,600,000 in the previous 12 months.		
The cash accounting scheme enables businesses to ignore the tax point rules and account for VAT only when it is paid and received.		

Task 1.9

The following tasks relate to your employer, Neo Bros' business.

Neo Bros uses annual accounting, and the business' VAT year is to 31 December.

The VAT liability for the previous year was £36,000.

You have the following information available, and you are asked to calculate your employer, Neo Bros', VAT payable to HMRC.

- Annual sales of standard-rated services were £201,000 excluding VAT.
- Staff wages outside the scope of VAT were £85,000.
- Standard-rated stationery purchases inclusive of VAT totalled £2,760.
- A new computer was bought for £1,800 inclusive of VAT at 20%.
- Zero-rated travel by employees on business cost £7,100.
- A car was purchased for business use costing £10,000 plus £2,000 VAT. The car is used by Neo Walker, the owner of the business, at weekends.
- £250 was donated to a local charity.

Required

(a) Complete the following table showing your workings where appropriate. If an answer is zero input 0.

	£	£
Output VAT		
Input VAT		
Wages		
Stationary		
Computer		
Travel		
Car		
Charity		
Total input VAT to deduct		
VAT payable		

(b) Complete the following sentences about the number, and amount, of payments on account under the annual accounting scheme for Neo Bros.

[▼] payments on account [▼] be made.

Each payment is [▼] of the previous years' VAT liability, being

£[▼] each.

Picklist
- 10%
- 3,000
- 4,000
- 90%
- May
- Must
- Nine
- Twelve

(c) Complete the following sentences about when the VAT payments will be made for Neo Bros under the annual accounting scheme.

The first payment is due in [▼] and then every month until [▼].

Any balance is due [▼] months after the VAT year end, along with the VAT return.

Picklist
- April
- December
- January
- One
- Two

(d) Which of the following statements about the annual accounting scheme are correct?

	✓
VAT-exclusive taxable turnover is not expected to exceed £1,350,000 in the next 12 months.	
VAT-inclusive taxable turnover is not expected to exceed £1,350,000 in the next 12 months.	
If VAT-exclusive taxable supplies exceed £1,600,000 at the end of the VAT accounting year, the business must leave the scheme.	
If VAT-inclusive taxable supplies exceed £1,600,000 at the end of the VAT accounting year, the business must leave the scheme.	

(e) Which of the following are disadvantages of the annual accounting scheme?

	✓
Submitting only one VAT return reduces the administrative burden of VAT.	
If turnover decreases, the interim payments may be higher than they need to be.	
The business will have to wait until the end of the year when it submits its return for a refund.	
The business has an extra month between the end of the VAT period and the return submission date.	

Neo Bros has heard there is alternative option to make payments on account under the annual accounting scheme.

Required

(f) Complete the following sentences using the picklists below.

A trader may alternatively opt for [▼] , [▼] payments of [▼] of the previous year's VAT liability.

These payments are due at the end of months [▼] , [▼] and [▼] in the VAT year.

The balance [▼] with the return as for traders who make nine, monthly payments.

Picklist

- 1
- 10
- 12
- 25%
- 4
- 50%
- 7
- Is due
- Is not due
- Monthly
- Quarterly
- Three
- Two

Task 1.10

You are Mira, a part-qualified accounting technician who works at A&T Ltd, an accounting firm.

A&T Ltd has recently taken on a new client, Jordan, who is starting a sole trader business. Jordan is opening a new furniture store and needs to employ staff to work in the business. She has come to you for some general advice around payroll.

Required

(a) Which TWO of the following statements are correct in relation to the use and functions of payroll software.

	✓
Once installed, payroll software will never need to be updated.	
Payroll software is used to provide information to HMRC under Real Time Information (RTI).	
Payroll software can calculate statutory maternity pay.	
All payroll software that is tested and approved by HRMC will be suitable for any business.	

(b) Use the picklists below to identify the function of the following payroll forms and returns.

Form	Function
Full Payment Submission (FPS)	▼
P11D	▼
P45	▼
P60	▼

Picklist
- Calculation of employer Class 1A NIC
- Details of employee leaving
- End of year summary of pay and deductions
- End of year summary of taxable benefits
- Return showing pay and deductions for each employee on a specific payment date

(c) Use the picklists below to complete the following sentences.

A Full Payment Submission (FPS) form must be filed with HMRC every [▼].

An Employer Payment Summary (EPS) must be filed every [▼] where no employees are paid.

Picklist
- Day
- Month
- Time employees are paid
- Year

(d) Identify whether the following statements concerning payroll records are true or false.

	True ✓	False ✓
A maximum penalty of £3,000 per year may apply for failure to maintain full records.		
HMRC may make an unannounced visit to an employer's premises to inspect payroll records.		
HMRC do not require employers to keep records of Payroll Giving Scheme documents.		
Records are required to be maintained for three years from the end of the relevant tax year to which they relate.		

The sentences below are concerning year end procedures.

Required

(e) Complete the following sentences using the picklists below.

The form P60 [▼] be provided to each employee by [▼] following the end of the [▼].

A copy of the form P11D [▼] be provided to the employee by [▼] following the end of the [▼].

A PAYE settlement agreement (PSA) is where the employer agrees to pay the employees' income tax on [▼].

Picklist
- 22 July
- 31 May
- 6 July
- Accounting year
- All benefits
- Any minor or irregular benefits
- May
- Must
- Tax year

Task 1.11

The following questions relate to the business of Roka Ltd.

You are Jeannie, a part-qualified accounting technician working in the tax department of Towers Ltd, an accounting firm.

Towers Ltd has recently taken on Roka Ltd as a new client. The directors at Roka Ltd are concerned that there may be some VAT errors and they would like your advice.

You discover that Roka Ltd recorded a purchase invoice as showing input VAT of £70 instead of the correct amount of £7.

In the same VAT period, Roka Ltd included a sales invoice with VAT of £400 twice in the sales day book.

Required

(a) Complete the table to show the net error.

	£
Output VAT overstated by	
Input VAT overstated by	
Net error	

Roka Ltd has turnover of £7 million.

The output VAT on its last return was understated by £57,000.

Required

(b) Which ONE of the following statements below is correct.

	✓
A correction cannot be made on the next return as the error exceeds £10,000.	
A correction can be made on the next VAT return as the error is less than 1% of turnover.	
A correction cannot be made on the next return as the error exceeds £50,000.	

The sentences below are concerning non-deliberate errors.

Required

(c) Complete the following sentences using the picklists below.

The error correction threshold is the [▼] of:

£[▼] and [▼] % of [▼], subject to an overall limit of £[▼].

Picklist

- 1
- 10
- 10,000
- 100,000
- 5
- 50,000
- Greater
- Lower
- Net VAT
- Turnover

28   EPA Knowledge Assessment

A director at Roka Ltd has asked you how a small understatement of input tax in a previous quarter, that is below the error correction threshold, would be dealt with on the VAT return.

Required

(d) Which ONE of the following is correct about how such an understatement would be shown on the VAT return?

	✓
It shouldn't be shown on the VAT return.	
It should be shown in box 1 of the VAT return.	
It should be shown in box 4 of the VAT return.	

The directors at Roka Ltd would like to briefly understand what happens when a VAT return is submitted late, or if a VAT liability is paid late.

Required

(e) Which of the following statements are correct about late submission of a VAT return.

	✓
If a VAT return is submitted late and there is no VAT due, there will be no penalty implications.	
Each time a taxpayer submits a VAT return late, this counts as a failure and each failure gets one penalty point.	
There is no financial penalty until the taxpayer reaches the penalty point threshold.	
Individual penalty points expire after one year.	

(f) State which of the following statements about late payment of VAT are true or false.

	True ✓	False ✓
If the VAT is paid late to HMRC, then no penalty is payable if the liability is settled within 15 days.		
If the VAT is outstanding after 15 days a penalty is charged at HMRC's discretion.		
If the VAT is outstanding after 15 days a penalty of 2% is charged on the amount outstanding.		
If the VAT is outstanding at the end of 30 days, a further 4% is charged per day.		
If the VAT is outstanding at the end of 30 days, a further 2% is charged, and from day 31 onwards 4% per annum is charged.		

The payroll manager at Roka Ltd has asked you about the implications of late submissions of payroll filings.

Required

(g) Complete the following sentence using the picklists below.

If a FPS is late, a penalty of between £[____▼____] and £[____▼____] per [____▼____] is imposed, depending on the number of [____▼____] the business has.

Picklist
- 100
- 200
- 400
- Employees
- Late submissions
- Month
- Quarter
- Transactions

Chapter 2 – Financial Accounting: Preparing Financial Statements (FAPS)

FAPS Summaries

The diagrams that follow are summaries from 'Financial Accounting: Preparing Financial Statements (FAPS)' covering the key areas most relevant to your EPA Knowledge assessment. The summaries and tasks included in this chapter are based on the AAT 'Scope of content – knowledge assessment' mapping contained in the AAT End Point Assessment Specification.

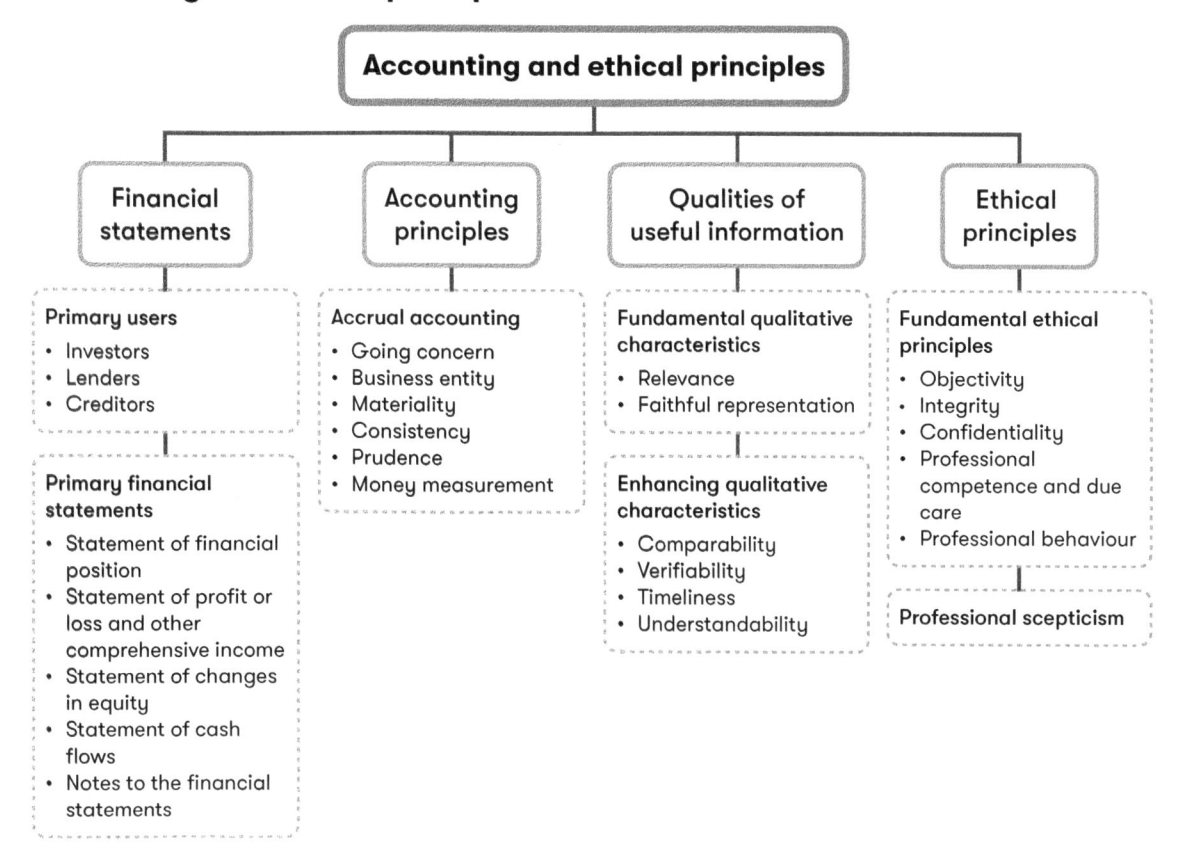

Accounting and ethical principles

Accounting and ethical principles

- **Financial statements**
  - Primary users
    - Investors
    - Lenders
    - Creditors
  - Primary financial statements
    - Statement of financial position
    - Statement of profit or loss and other comprehensive income
    - Statement of changes in equity
    - Statement of cash flows
    - Notes to the financial statements

- **Accounting principles**
  - Accrual accounting
    - Going concern
    - Business entity
    - Materiality
    - Consistency
    - Prudence
    - Money measurement

- **Qualities of useful information**
  - Fundamental qualitative characteristics
    - Relevance
    - Faithful representation
  - Enhancing qualitative characteristics
    - Comparability
    - Verifiability
    - Timeliness
    - Understandability

- **Ethical principles**
  - Fundamental ethical principles
    - Objectivity
    - Integrity
    - Confidentiality
    - Professional competence and due care
    - Professional behaviour
  - Professional scepticism

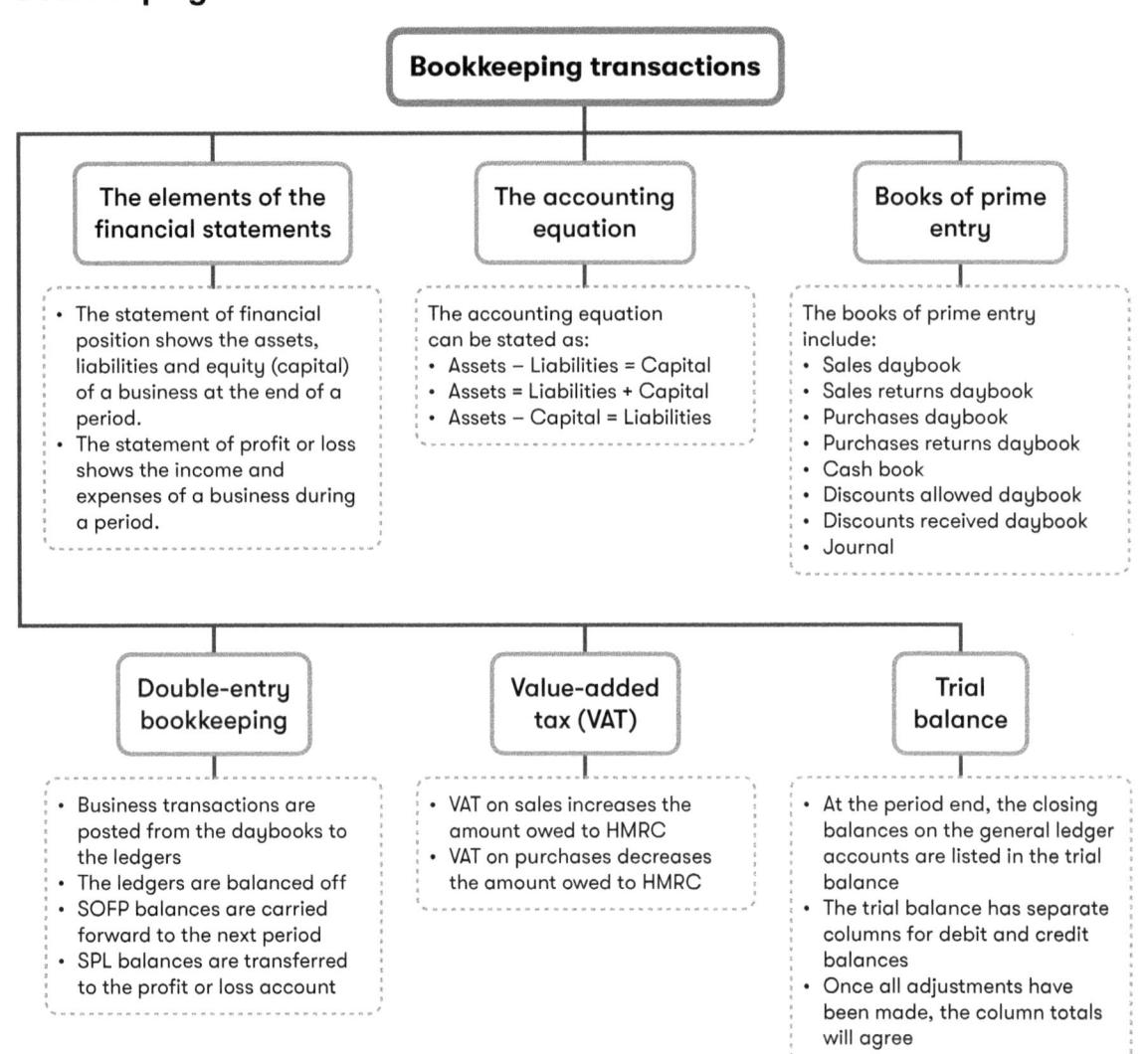

Bookkeeping transactions

Bookkeeping transactions

The elements of the financial statements
- The statement of financial position shows the assets, liabilities and equity (capital) of a business at the end of a period.
- The statement of profit or loss shows the income and expenses of a business during a period.

The accounting equation
The accounting equation can be stated as:
- Assets – Liabilities = Capital
- Assets = Liabilities + Capital
- Assets – Capital = Liabilities

Books of prime entry
The books of prime entry include:
- Sales daybook
- Sales returns daybook
- Purchases daybook
- Purchases returns daybook
- Cash book
- Discounts allowed daybook
- Discounts received daybook
- Journal

Double-entry bookkeeping
- Business transactions are posted from the daybooks to the ledgers
- The ledgers are balanced off
- SOFP balances are carried forward to the next period
- SPL balances are transferred to the profit or loss account

Value-added tax (VAT)
- VAT on sales increases the amount owed to HMRC
- VAT on purchases decreases the amount owed to HMRC

Trial balance
- At the period end, the closing balances on the general ledger accounts are listed in the trial balance
- The trial balance has separate columns for debit and credit balances
- Once all adjustments have been made, the column totals will agree

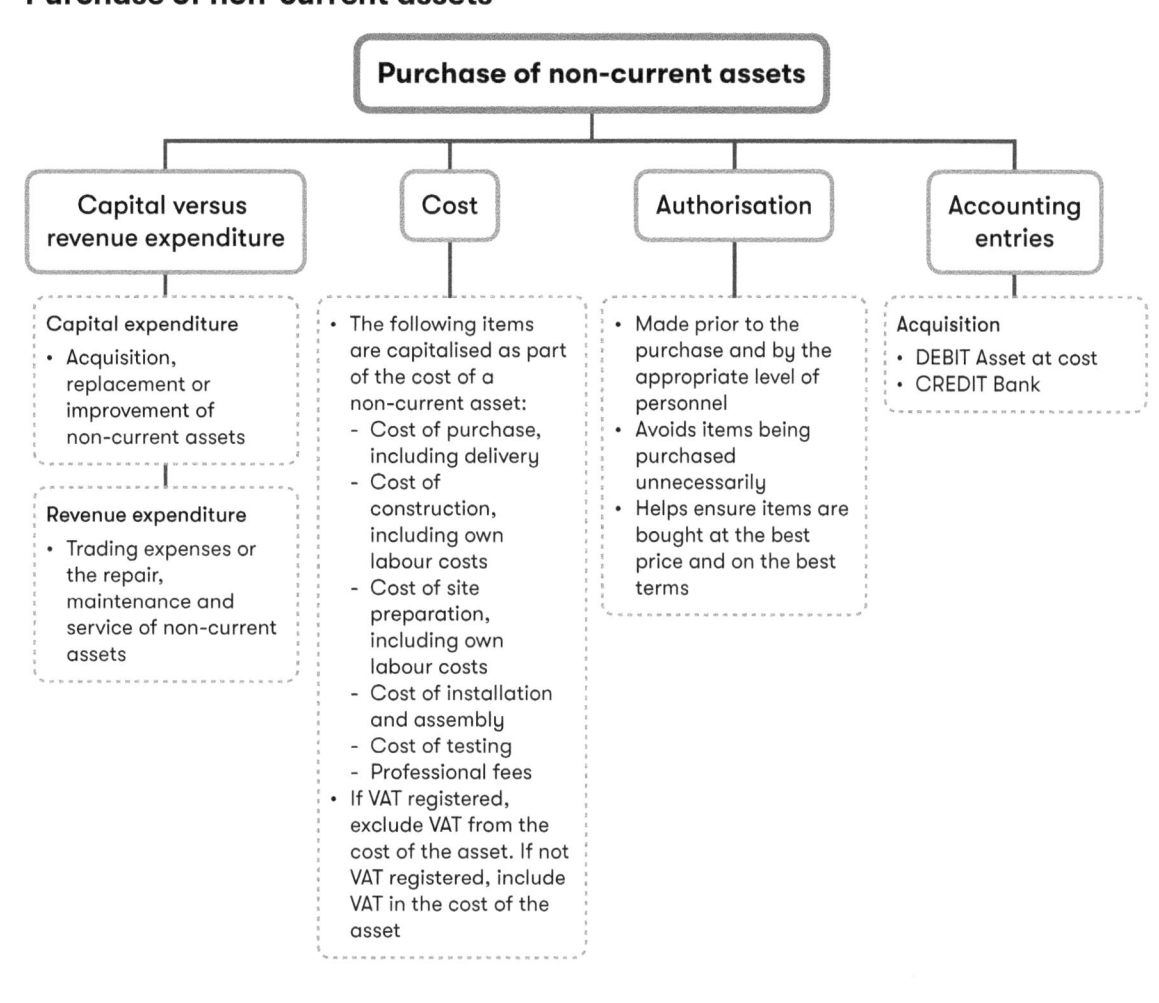

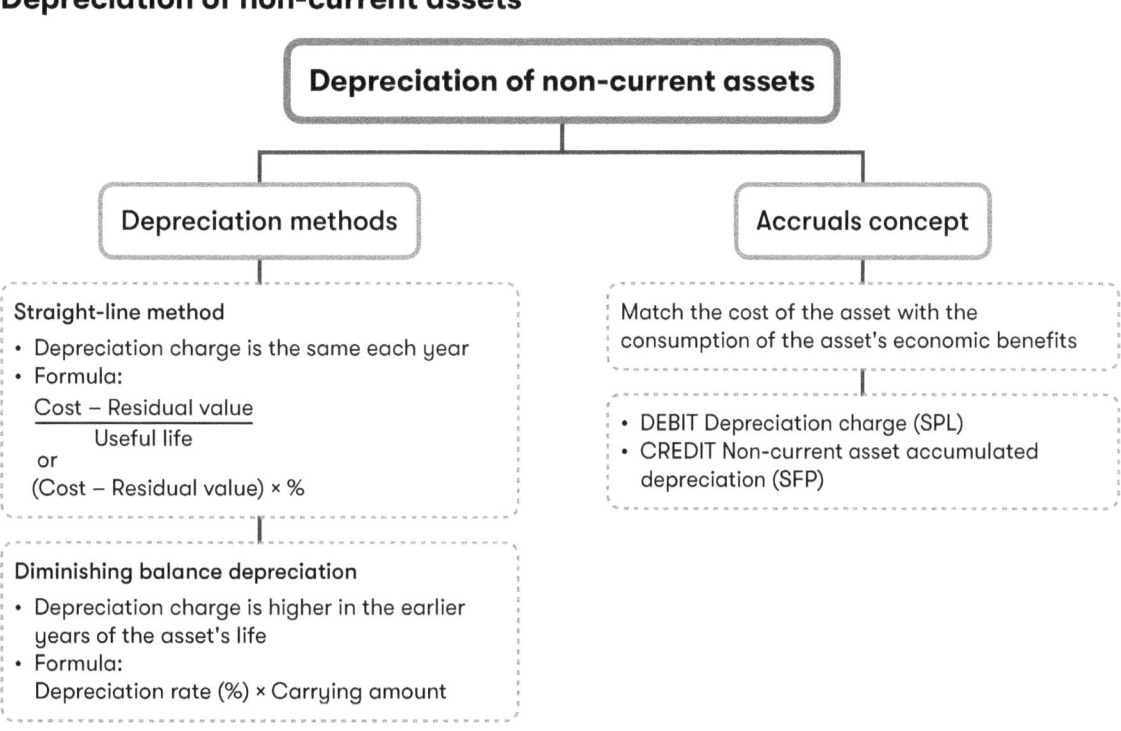

Purchase of non-current assets

Purchase of non-current assets

Capital versus revenue expenditure

Capital expenditure
- Acquisition, replacement or improvement of non-current assets

Revenue expenditure
- Trading expenses or the repair, maintenance and service of non-current assets

Cost

- The following items are capitalised as part of the cost of a non-current asset:
  - Cost of purchase, including delivery
  - Cost of construction, including own labour costs
  - Cost of site preparation, including own labour costs
  - Cost of installation and assembly
  - Cost of testing
  - Professional fees
- If VAT registered, exclude VAT from the cost of the asset. If not VAT registered, include VAT in the cost of the asset

Authorisation

- Made prior to the purchase and by the appropriate level of personnel
- Avoids items being purchased unnecessarily
- Helps ensure items are bought at the best price and on the best terms

Accounting entries

Acquisition
- DEBIT Asset at cost
- CREDIT Bank

Depreciation of non-current assets

Depreciation of non-current assets

Depreciation methods

Straight-line method
- Depreciation charge is the same each year
- Formula:
  $$\frac{\text{Cost} - \text{Residual value}}{\text{Useful life}}$$
  or
  (Cost − Residual value) × %

Diminishing balance depreciation
- Depreciation charge is higher in the earlier years of the asset's life
- Formula:
  Depreciation rate (%) × Carrying amount

Accruals concept

Match the cost of the asset with the consumption of the asset's economic benefits

- DEBIT Depreciation charge (SPL)
- CREDIT Non-current asset accumulated depreciation (SFP)

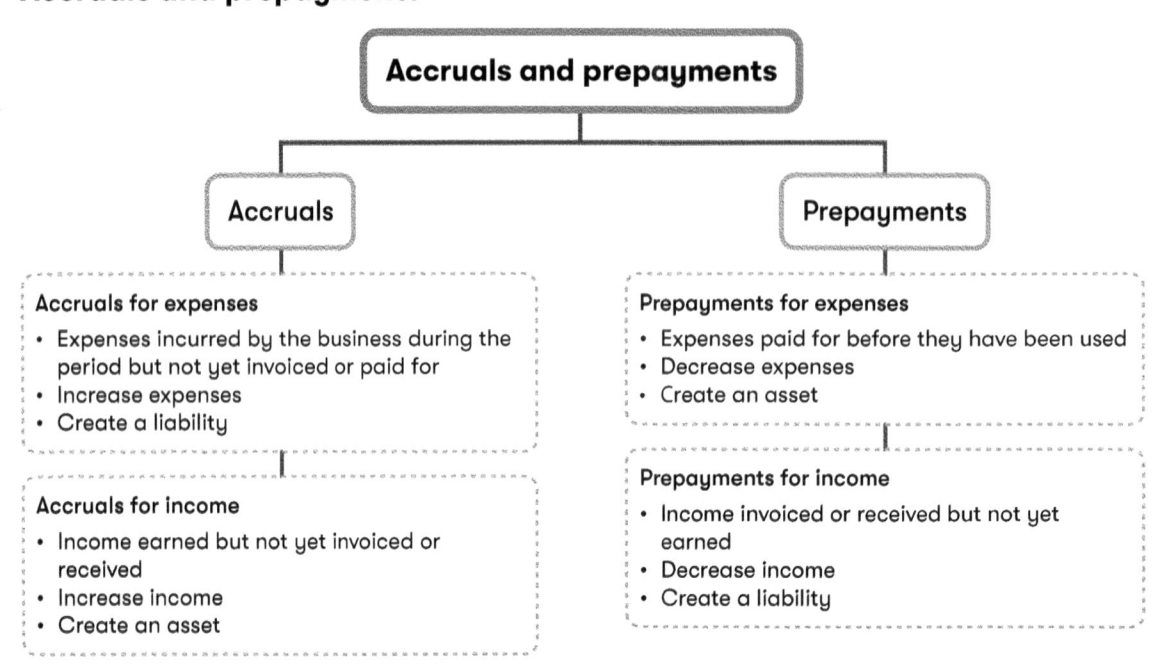

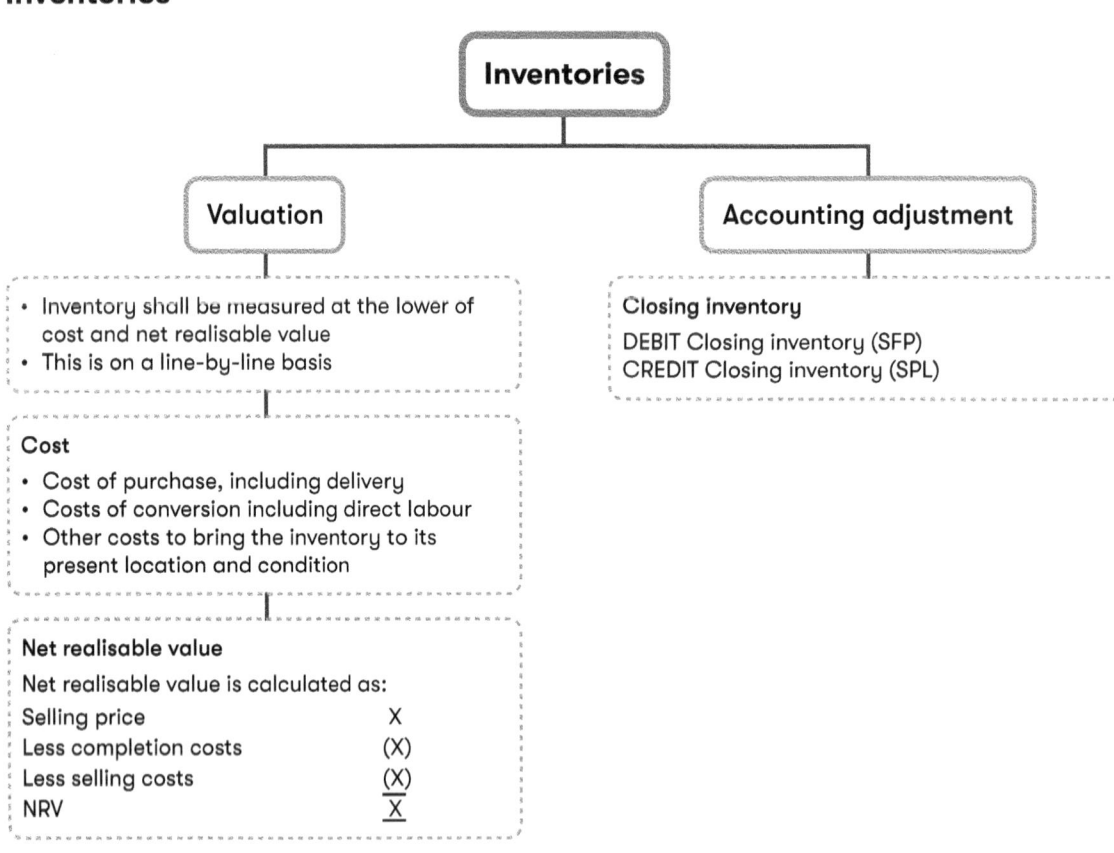

Accruals and prepayments

Accruals and prepayments

Accruals

Accruals for expenses
- Expenses incurred by the business during the period but not yet invoiced or paid for
- Increase expenses
- Create a liability

Accruals for income
- Income earned but not yet invoiced or received
- Increase income
- Create an asset

Prepayments

Prepayments for expenses
- Expenses paid for before they have been used
- Decrease expenses
- Create an asset

Prepayments for income
- Income invoiced or received but not yet earned
- Decrease income
- Create a liability

Inventories

Inventories

Valuation

- Inventory shall be measured at the lower of cost and net realisable value
- This is on a line-by-line basis

Cost
- Cost of purchase, including delivery
- Costs of conversion including direct labour
- Other costs to bring the inventory to its present location and condition

Net realisable value

Net realisable value is calculated as:

Selling price	X
Less completion costs	(X)
Less selling costs	(X)
NRV	X

Accounting adjustment

Closing inventory

DEBIT Closing inventory (SFP)
CREDIT Closing inventory (SPL)

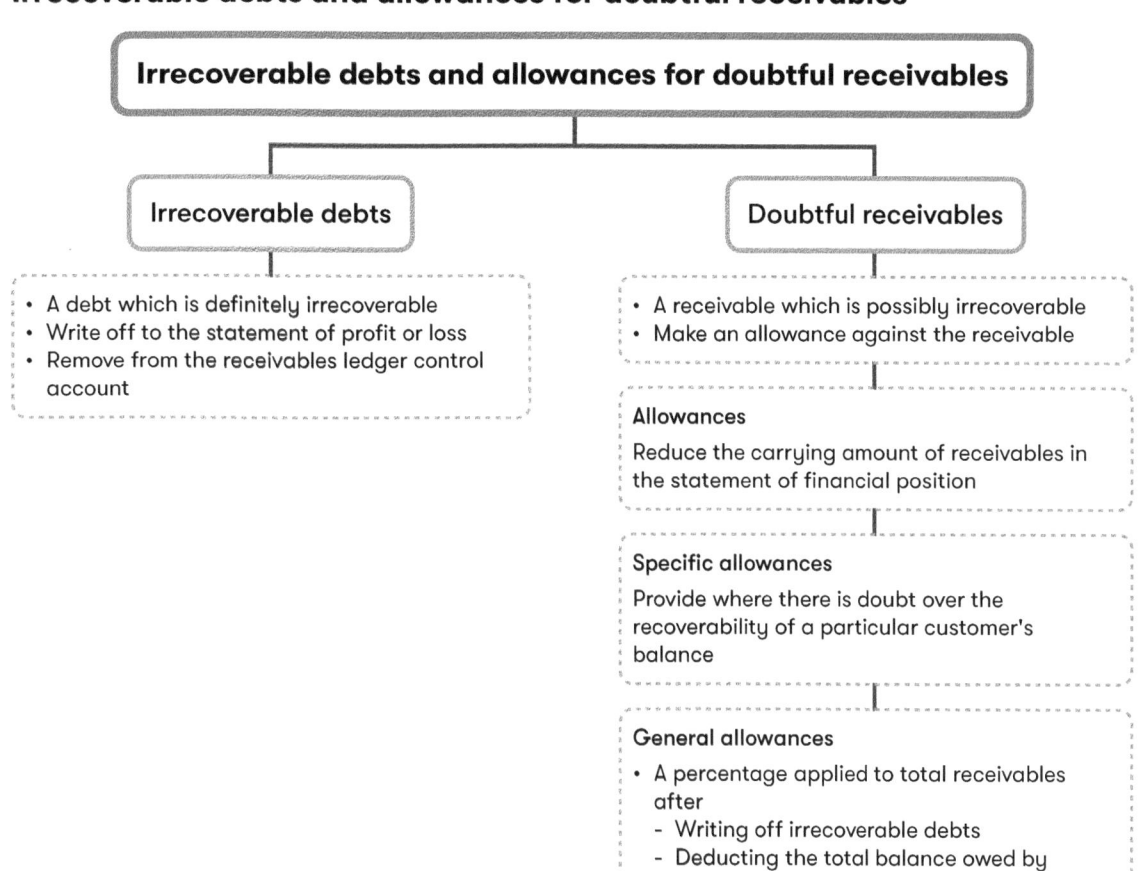

Irrecoverable debts and allowances for doubtful receivables

Irrecoverable debts and allowances for doubtful receivables

Irrecoverable debts

- A debt which is definitely irrecoverable
- Write off to the statement of profit or loss
- Remove from the receivables ledger control account

Doubtful receivables

- A receivable which is possibly irrecoverable
- Make an allowance against the receivable

Allowances

Reduce the carrying amount of receivables in the statement of financial position

Specific allowances

Provide where there is doubt over the recoverability of a particular customer's balance

General allowances

- A percentage applied to total receivables after
  - Writing off irrecoverable debts
  - Deducting the total balance owed by customers where a specific allowance has been made
- The general allowance is increased or decreased as necessary at each year end

Bank reconciliations

Bank reconciliations

Cash book balance
Business's record of the amount of cash held by the business at a point in time

Bank statement balance
Bank's record of the amount of cash held by the business at a point in time

Differences
Due to:
- Timing differences (adjust balance per bank statement)
    - Unrecorded lodgements
    - Outstanding cheques
- Cash book needs to be updated (adjust cash book) eg
    - Standing orders
    - Direct debits
    - BACS transfers
    - Bank charges
    - Interest
    - Counter credits
    - Faster payments
- Bank errors

Control account reconciliations

Control account reconciliations

Reconciliations

Receivables ledger control account (RLCA)
The total owed by all credit customers at a particular point in time

Payables ledger control account (PLCA)
The total owed to all credit suppliers at a particular point in time

Subsidiary receivables ledger (RL)
Individual accounts listing transactions with each credit customer

Subsidiary payables ledger (PL)
Individual accounts listing transactions with each credit supplier

The RLCA and the RL, and the PLCA and the PL show the same information and so the balances should reconcile

Other considerations

Contra entries
- May be made when a business has a customer which is also a supplier
- A contra will always be for the lower of the two amounts owed
- Contra entries reduce the balances in the receivables ledger control account and payables ledger control account

Discounts allowed and received
- Discounts allowed are offered by a business to their credit customer (an expense)
- Discounts received are received by a business from their suppliers (sundry income)

Payroll

- Payroll transactions are recorded using the usual principles of double entry
- The general ledger accounts used to record payroll transactions include:
  - Wages control account
  - Wages expense
  - HMRC

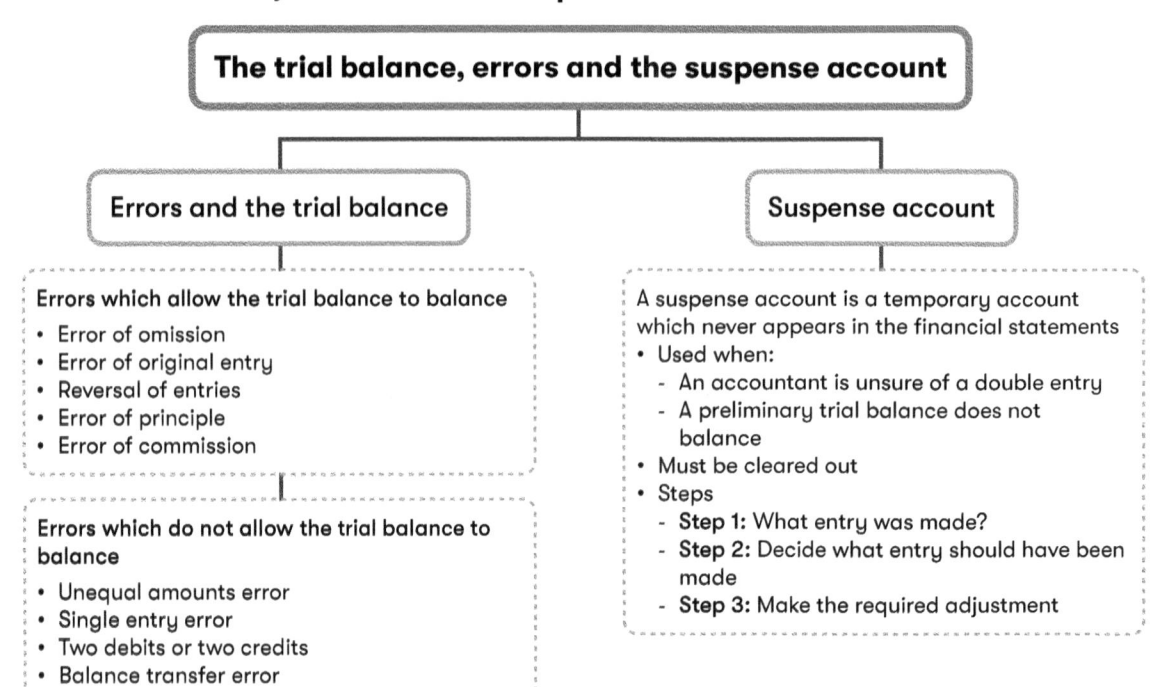

The trial balance, errors and the suspense account

The trial balance, errors and the suspense account

Errors and the trial balance

Errors which allow the trial balance to balance
- Error of omission
- Error of original entry
- Reversal of entries
- Error of principle
- Error of commission

Errors which do not allow the trial balance to balance
- Unequal amounts error
- Single entry error
- Two debits or two credits
- Balance transfer error

Suspense account

A suspense account is a temporary account which never appears in the financial statements
- Used when:
  - An accountant is unsure of a double entry
  - A preliminary trial balance does not balance
- Must be cleared out
- Steps
  - **Step 1:** What entry was made?
  - **Step 2:** Decide what entry should have been made
  - **Step 3:** Make the required adjustment

Incomplete records

Incomplete records

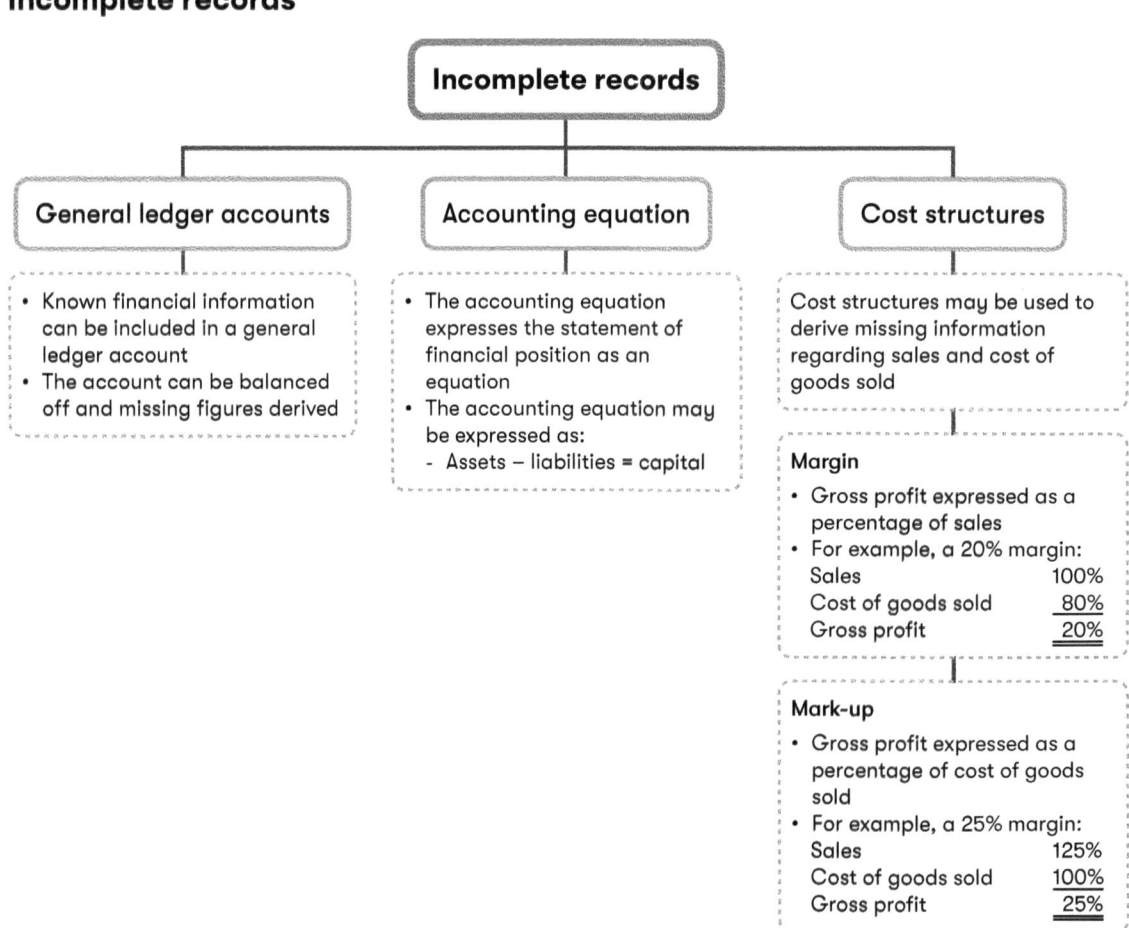

General ledger accounts
- Known financial information can be included in a general ledger account
- The account can be balanced off and missing figures derived

Accounting equation
- The accounting equation expresses the statement of financial position as an equation
- The accounting equation may be expressed as:
  - Assets – liabilities = capital

Cost structures

Cost structures may be used to derive missing information regarding sales and cost of goods sold

Margin
- Gross profit expressed as a percentage of sales
- For example, a 20% margin:

Sales	100%
Cost of goods sold	80%
Gross profit	20%

Mark-up
- Gross profit expressed as a percentage of cost of goods sold
- For example, a 25% margin:

Sales	125%
Cost of goods sold	100%
Gross profit	25%

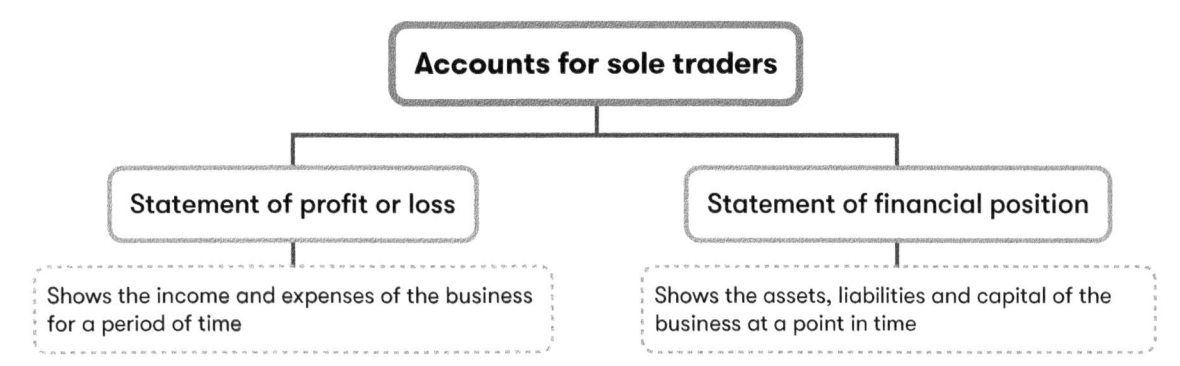

Accounts for sole traders

```
                    ┌─────────────────────────────┐
                    │  Accounts for sole traders  │
                    └──────────────┬──────────────┘
                    ┌──────────────┴──────────────┐
        ┌───────────────────────┐      ┌───────────────────────────────┐
        │ Statement of profit   │      │ Statement of financial        │
        │ or loss               │      │ position                      │
        └───────────┬───────────┘      └───────────────┬───────────────┘
        ┌───────────────────────┐      ┌───────────────────────────────┐
        │ Shows the income and  │      │ Shows the assets, liabilities │
        │ expenses of the       │      │ and capital of the business   │
        │ business for a        │      │ at a point in time            │
        │ period of time        │      │                               │
        └───────────────────────┘      └───────────────────────────────┘
```

FAPS Practice Tasks

Task 2.1

Select the correct accounting principle that matches each description.

Accounting concept	Description
A transaction should only be included in the final accounts if it can be measured in monetary terms.	▼
Applying the same methods to account for the same or similar items, from period to period within a reporting entity which helps to ensure that information is comparable over time.	▼
The exercise of caution when making judgements so that assets, income and profits are not overstated and liabilities, expenses and losses are not understated.	▼

Picklist
- Business entity
- Consistency
- Going concern
- Materiality
- Money measurement
- Prudence

Task 2.2

Select the correct accounting principle that matches each description.

Accounting concept	Description
Income and expenses shown in the statement of profit or loss are those that were earned or incurred during the period rather than the cash received or paid in the period.	▼
Omitting, misstating or obscuring information that could reasonably be expected to influence the decisions made by the primary users.	▼
The financial statements are normally prepared on the assumption that an entity will continue in operation for the foreseeable future.	▼

Picklist
- Accrual accounting
- Business entity
- Consistency
- Going concern
- Materiality
- Money measurement
- Prudence

Task 2.3

Complete the following sentence by selecting the correct option.

Confirmatory value and predictive value enable financial information to be [▼] in making a difference to the decisions made by users.

Picklist
- Comparable
- Faithfully represented
- Relevant
- Verifiable

Task 2.4

In which TWO of the following circumstances would it be appropriate to disclose information about your client (or company) without breaching the fundamental principle of confidentiality?

	✓
Your manager asks to review your year-end accounting work in relation to the client (or company).	
Another client (or company) asks for details because they want to approach the client (or company) about purchasing their business.	
The client's bank requests to see the financial statements and your client has granted permission.	
A friend wants details on the financial situation of your client (or company) because they are considering purchasing shares in the client (company).	

Task 2.5

Classify each of the following general ledger accounts according to where they would be presented in the financial statements.

General ledger account	Financial statement classification
Cost of intangible assets	▼
Bank overdraft	▼
Long term bank loan account	▼
Inventory	▼
Sales	▼

Picklist
- Capital
- Current assets
- Current liabilities
- Distribution expenses
- Income
- Non-current assets
- Non-current liabilities

Task 2.6

Select the appropriate daybook from the picklist to indicate where the different transactions are recorded.

Invoices received from suppliers	▼
Invoices issued to customers	▼
Credit notes received from suppliers	▼
Credit notes issued to customers	▼

Picklist
- Cash book
- Purchases daybook
- Purchases returns daybook
- Sales daybook
- Sales returns daybook

Task 2.7

Indicate whether the following statements are true or false.

(a) The VAT control account can be either a credit or debit balance at the period end.

	✓
True	
False	

(b) The payables ledger control account and receivables ledger control account contain summarised totals of all the individual transactions affecting their respective ledgers.

	✓
True	
False	

(c) The receivables and payables memorandum (subsidiary) accounts form part of the double entry system.

	✓
True	
False	

(d) At the end of a period, once all the necessary payroll entries have been made the wages control will reflect the wages expense for the period.

	✓
True	
False	

Task 2.8

Accounting software can help to automate accounting processes.

Required

Which TWO of the following are true in respect of automation.

	✓
Accounting software will often automatically transfer data or totals to control accounts based on individual entries made throughout the period.	
If accounting software is used to automate a process, then there is no need to review or check the results.	
It is not possible to automate any processes associated with non-current assets.	
Accounting packages can automate the process of updating the control accounts and subsidiary ledgers at the same time to minimise the probability of any differences arising.	

Task 2.9

You are preparing the plant and machinery cost account.

The account had a balance of £40,246 at the beginning of the period. The cash book figure for the year is £522,730.

Required

Complete the plant and machinery cost account ensuring it is balanced off appropriately.

Plant and machinery cost account

	£		£
▼		▼	
▼		▼	
Total		Total	

Picklist

- Balance b/d
- Balance c/d
- Capital
- Cash book
- Profit and loss account

Task 2.10

Company B buys a new property for £1,000,000. Other costs related to purchase are:

- Legal completion costs of £30,000.
- A payment to the conveyancing solicitor of £4,600 for their work on the property purchase.
- Late in the period, the business had to carry out some repairs to the roof on the property at a cost of £17,400.

You may ignore VAT in this task.

The business will credit the bank general ledger account for the £1,052,000 spent during the period.

Required

Ignoring depreciation, what is the impact of recording the debit side of the above transactions on the business's statement of financial position and statement of profit or loss for the period?

Description	Impact	Amount £
Statement of financial position	▼	
Statement of profit or loss	▼	

Picklist

- Increase current assets
- Increase current liabilities
- Increase non-current assets
- Increase profit
- No impact
- Reduce profit

Task 2.11

Company C has an authorisation policy in place for purchases of any non-current assets.

Organisational policy is that the authorisation levels are as follows:

- Assets costing less than £1,000 – Supervisor
- Assets costing between £1,000 and £5,000 – Manager
- Assets costing over £5,000 – Company Director

An assistant has expressed a need to purchase new equipment costing £1,200.

Required

Which TWO of the following roles can authorise this purchase?

	✓
Assistant requesting the equipment	
Supervisor	
Manager	
Company Director	

Task 2.12

Which TWO the following statements relating to the non-current assets register is true?

	✓
The non-current asset register is always maintained separately and independently from the information in the accounting software.	
Postings for depreciation are only made in the general ledger but not in the non-current asset register.	
Acquisitions and disposals need to be reflected in both the general ledger and non-current asset register.	
A control adopted by companies to help detect errors is to periodically reconcile the non-current asset register to the relevant general ledger accounts.	

Task 2.13

Company C, a VAT registered company, purchased new plant and equipment during the accounting period with a list price of £59,400 plus VAT. The company traded in old equipment as part exchange. The old equipment had a cost of £43,800 and accumulated depreciation of £5,586 at the date of part exchange.

A part exchange allowance of £33,600 was given in respect of the old equipment. The balance was paid using a bank transfer.

Required

(a) Complete the following sentence.

The company made a [▼] of £ [   ] on the part exchanged asset.

Picklist
- Loss on disposal
- Profit on disposal

(b) Calculate amount of the bank transfer made during the purchase of the new equipment.

£ [   ]

Task 2.14

You have been asked to calculate the depreciation for some specialist equipment owned by Company D. The diminishing balance method at a rate of 20% should be used. The company charges a full year of depreciation in the year of acquisition and none in the year of disposal.

The cost of the equipment is £155,016 and the accumulated depreciation at the start of the period is £30,756. There have been no additions or disposals during the year.

Required

(a) Calculate the depreciation charge for the year.

£ [   ]

(b) **Identify the journal that will be used to record the depreciation charge for the year.**

Debit [　　　▼　]

Credit [　　　▼　]

Picklist
- Accumulated depreciation
- Depreciation expense
- Disposals
- Equipment cost

Task 2.15

You are working on the accounting records of a business for the year ended 31 March 20X4 and considering accruals and prepayments.

You are looking into rent expenses for the year.

- At 31 March 20X3, there was a prepayment for rent expenses of £3,000.
- The cash book for the year shows payments for rent of £45,000.
- The amount paid includes £8,000 for the 6 months ended 30 June 20X4.

Required

(a) **Complete the prepaid expenses account.**

Prepaid expenses

	£		£
Balance b/d		▼	
▼		▼	
Total		Total	

Picklist
- Balance b/d
- Balance c/d
- Rent expense

An accrued expense needs to be recorded in respect of an invoice received after the end of the accounting period but relating to the current financial year.

Required

(b) **Complete the following statement.**

The adjustment to record the accrued expense will [　　　▼　] current liabilities in the statement of financial position.

Picklist
- Decrease
- Have no effect on
- Increase

Task 2.16

At the start of the accounting period, company G had an allowance for doubtful receivables of £10,000.

During the period, one customer owing £4,000 went into administration and the receivable was correctly written off as it was considered irrecoverable.

At the end of the year there is a balance on the receivables ledger control account of £100,000. Your manager estimates that 6% of this will not be paid.

Required

Complete the following sentence.

The balance for the allowance for doubtful receivables is £ ☐ .

Task 2.17

A business has 250 units of a product in inventory which cost £49.20 per unit plus £1.00 per unit of delivery costs. These goods can be sold for £51.60 per unit but in order to do this, selling costs of £2.00 per unit must be incurred.

Required

(a) What is the total cost per unit?

£ ☐

(b) What is the net realisable value of each unit?

£ ☐

(c) At what amount should the 250 units of the product be included in the closing inventory in the financial statements?

£ ☐

Task 2.18

You have been asked to look into problems found with the payables ledger reconciliation to the payables ledger control account.

Required

Which TWO of the following errors will be adjusted in the payables ledger control account.

	✓
Payments made to suppliers not reflected in the payables ledger control account entries.	
A supplier missing from the list of suppliers in the subsidiary payables ledger.	
A credit note entered on the wrong side of a suppliers account in the subsidiary ledger.	
An incorrect total posted to payables ledger control account.	

Task 2.19

The suspense account currently has a zero balance. A colleague says that must mean the financial statements are free from errors.

Required

Is the statement by your colleague true or false?

	✓
True	
False	

Task 2.20

You are comparing the bank statement with the cash book.

Required

Unpresented cheques are normally a cash book adjustment.

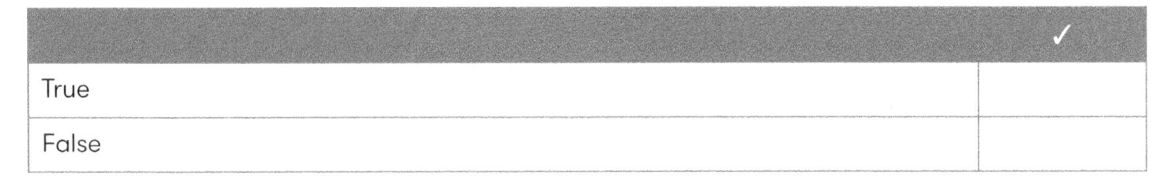

	✓
True	
False	

Task 2.21

Complete the following sentences about the financial statements.

The [▼] provide(s) a summary of the income and expenses incurred by the business over a period of time.

The [▼] list(s) all of the assets, liabilities and capital of the business on the period-end date of the accounting period.

Picklist
- Books of prime entry
- Control accounts
- Statement of financial position
- Statement of profit or loss

Task 2.22

For the year ended 31 March 20X4, a business has cost of goods sold of £520,000. The business has a mark-up on cost of 30%.

Required

What are the sales for the year ended 31 March 20X4?

£ [   ]

Chapter 3 – Management Accounting Techniques (MATS)

MATS Summaries

The diagrams that follow are summaries from 'Management Accounting Techniques (MATS)' covering the key areas most relevant to your EPA Knowledge assessment. The summaries and tasks included in this chapter are based on the AAT 'Scope of content – knowledge assessment' mapping contained in the AAT End Point Assessment Specification.

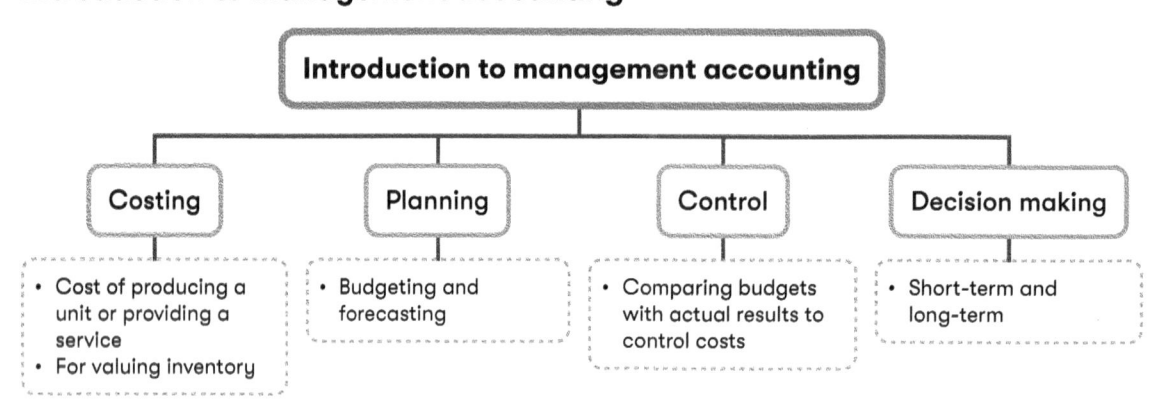

Introduction to management accounting

Introduction to management accounting

- **Costing**
  - Cost of producing a unit or providing a service
  - For valuing inventory
- **Planning**
  - Budgeting and forecasting
- **Control**
  - Comparing budgets with actual results to control costs
- **Decision making**
  - Short-term and long-term

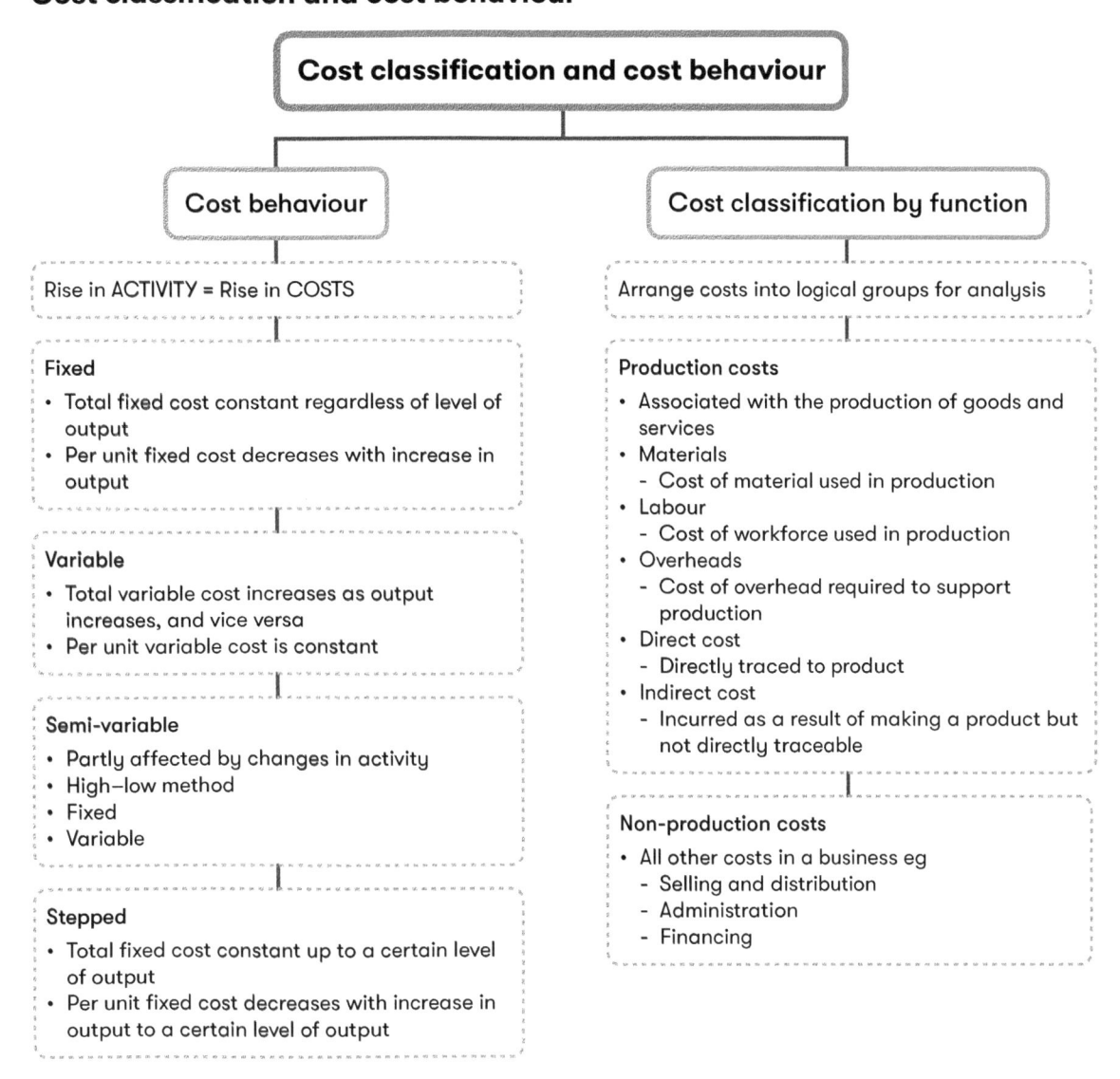

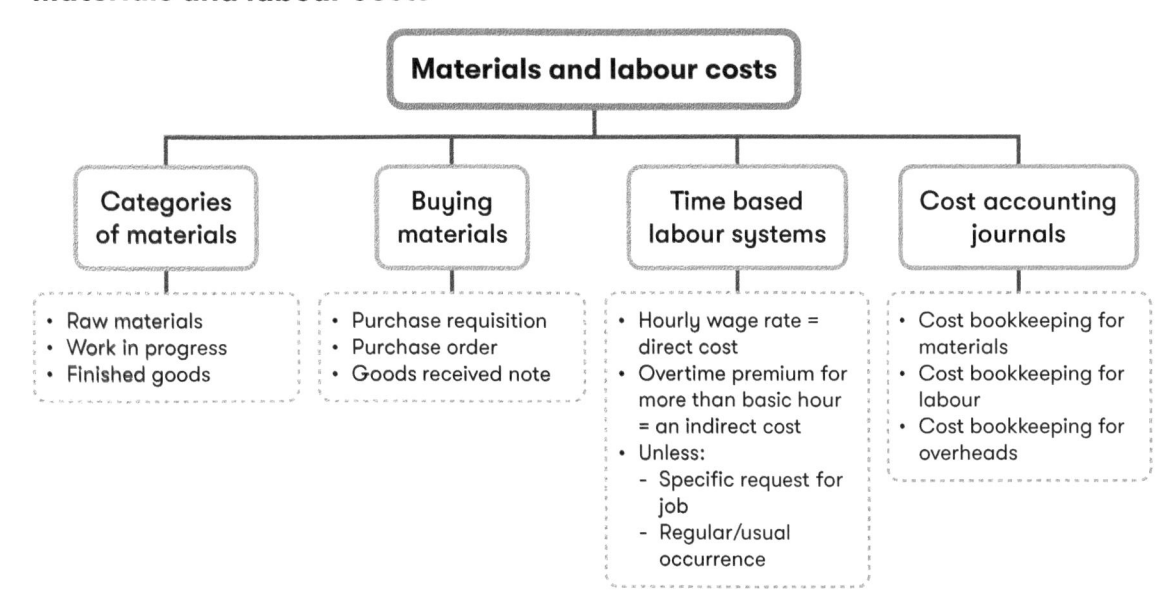

Cost classification and cost behaviour

Cost classification and cost behaviour

Cost behaviour

Rise in ACTIVITY = Rise in COSTS

Fixed
- Total fixed cost constant regardless of level of output
- Per unit fixed cost decreases with increase in output

Variable
- Total variable cost increases as output increases, and vice versa
- Per unit variable cost is constant

Semi-variable
- Partly affected by changes in activity
- High–low method
- Fixed
- Variable

Stepped
- Total fixed cost constant up to a certain level of output
- Per unit fixed cost decreases with increase in output to a certain level of output

Cost classification by function

Arrange costs into logical groups for analysis

Production costs
- Associated with the production of goods and services
- Materials
  - Cost of material used in production
- Labour
  - Cost of workforce used in production
- Overheads
  - Cost of overhead required to support production
- Direct cost
  - Directly traced to product
- Indirect cost
  - Incurred as a result of making a product but not directly traceable

Non-production costs
- All other costs in a business eg
  - Selling and distribution
  - Administration
  - Financing

Materials and labour costs

Materials and labour costs

Categories of materials
- Raw materials
- Work in progress
- Finished goods

Buying materials
- Purchase requisition
- Purchase order
- Goods received note

Time based labour systems
- Hourly wage rate = direct cost
- Overtime premium for more than basic hour = an indirect cost
- Unless:
  - Specific request for job
  - Regular/usual occurrence

Cost accounting journals
- Cost bookkeeping for materials
- Cost bookkeeping for labour
- Cost bookkeeping for overheads

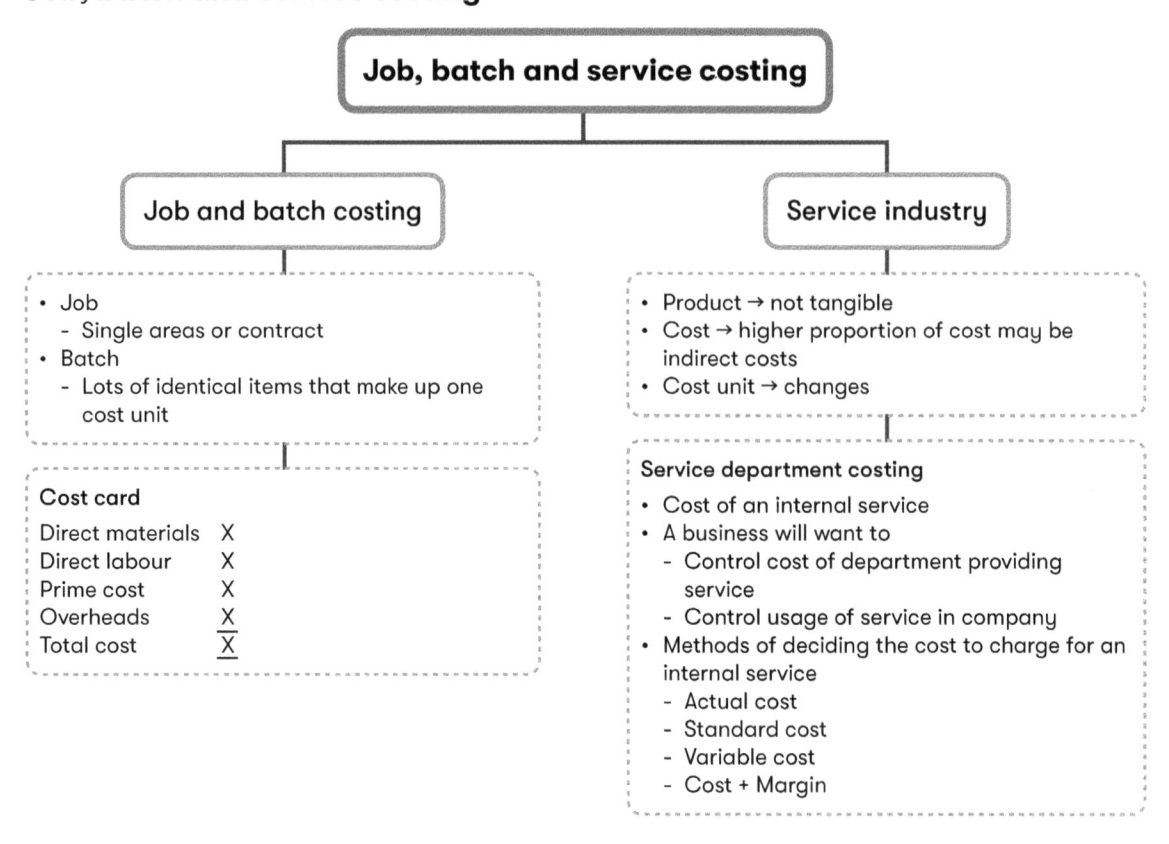

Job, batch and service costing

Job, batch and service costing

Job and batch costing

- Job
  - Single areas or contract
- Batch
  - Lots of identical items that make up one cost unit

Cost card

Direct materials	X
Direct labour	X
Prime cost	X
Overheads	X
Total cost	X

Service industry

- Product → not tangible
- Cost → higher proportion of cost may be indirect costs
- Cost unit → changes

Service department costing

- Cost of an internal service
- A business will want to
  - Control cost of department providing service
  - Control usage of service in company
- Methods of deciding the cost to charge for an internal service
  - Actual cost
  - Standard cost
  - Variable cost
  - Cost + Margin

Standard costing and budgeting

Standard costing and budgeting

Planning and control

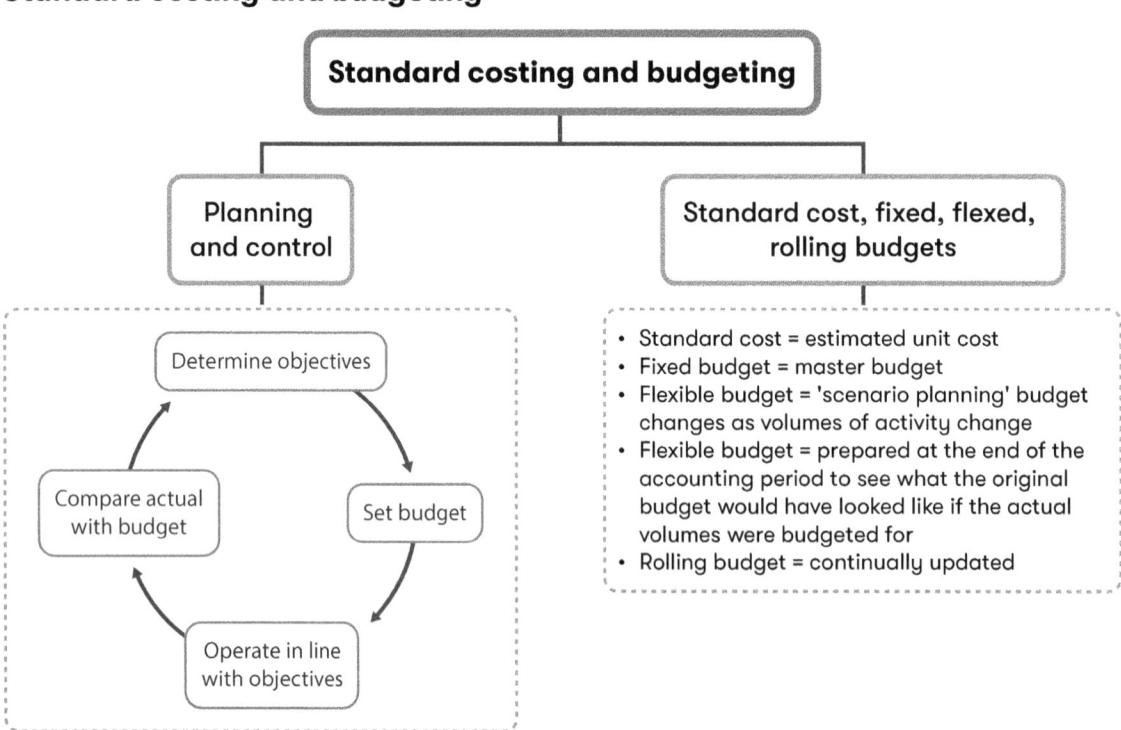

- Determine objectives
- Set budget
- Operate in line with objectives
- Compare actual with budget

Standard cost, fixed, flexed, rolling budgets

- Standard cost = estimated unit cost
- Fixed budget = master budget
- Flexible budget = 'scenario planning' budget changes as volumes of activity change
- Flexible budget = prepared at the end of the accounting period to see what the original budget would have looked like if the actual volumes were budgeted for
- Rolling budget = continually updated

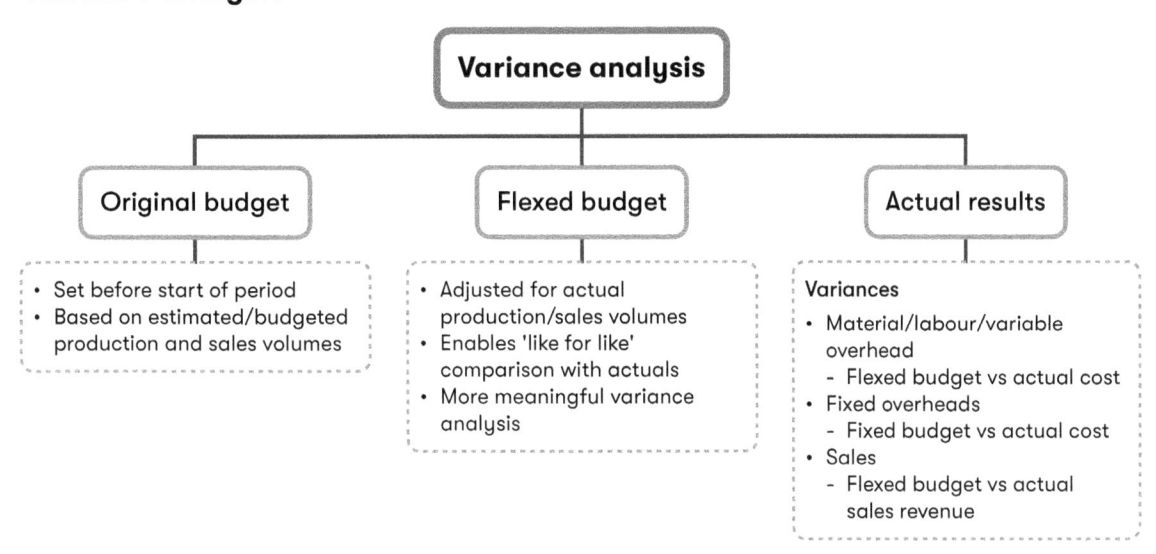

Variance analysis

Variance analysis

Original budget
- Set before start of period
- Based on estimated/budgeted production and sales volumes

Flexed budget
- Adjusted for actual production/sales volumes
- Enables 'like for like' comparison with actuals
- More meaningful variance analysis

Actual results
Variances
- Material/labour/variable overhead
  - Flexed budget vs actual cost
- Fixed overheads
  - Fixed budget vs actual cost
- Sales
  - Flexed budget vs actual sales revenue

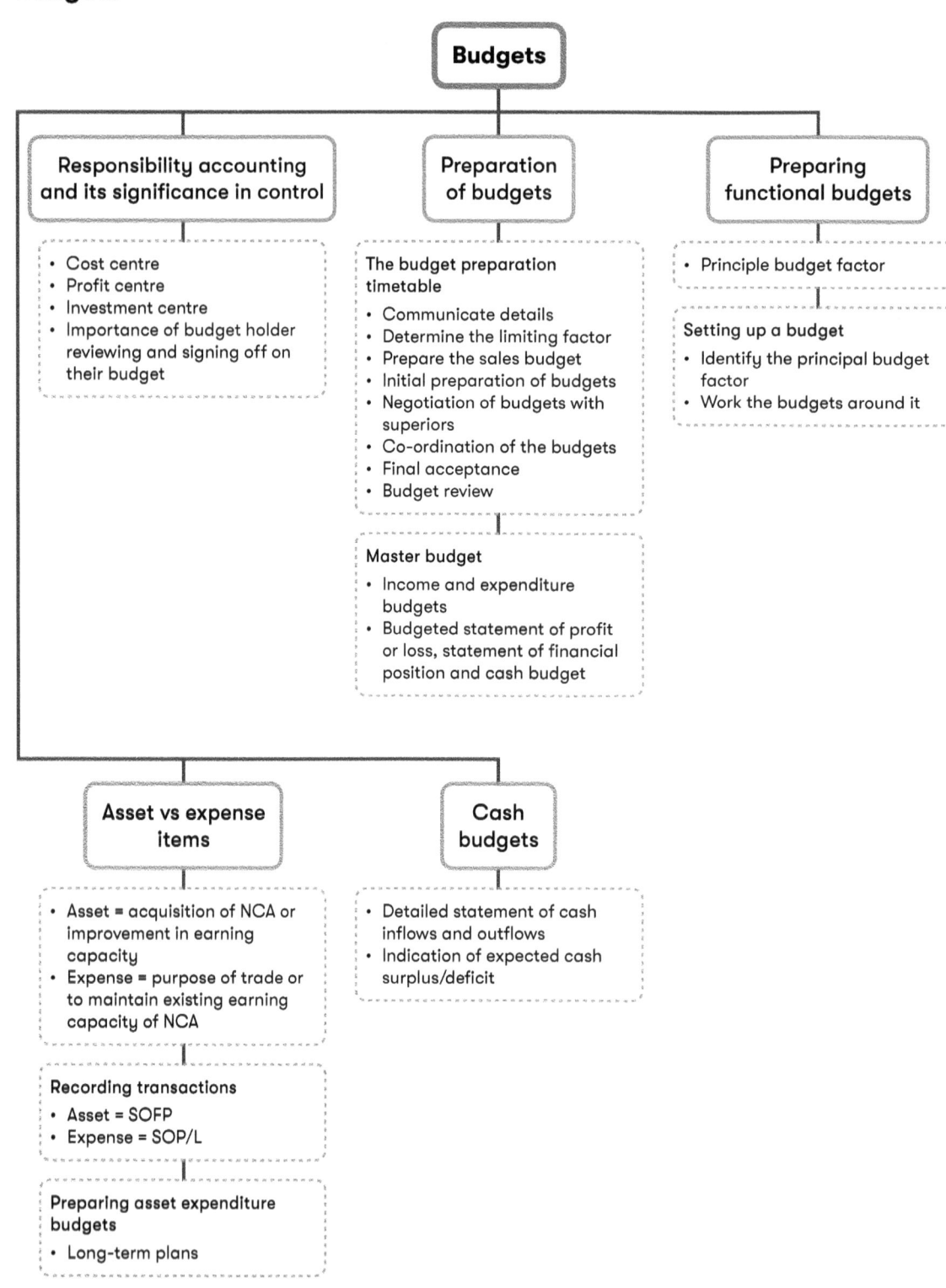

Budgets

Budgets

Responsibility accounting and its significance in control

- Cost centre
- Profit centre
- Investment centre
- Importance of budget holder reviewing and signing off on their budget

Preparation of budgets

The budget preparation timetable
- Communicate details
- Determine the limiting factor
- Prepare the sales budget
- Initial preparation of budgets
- Negotiation of budgets with superiors
- Co-ordination of the budgets
- Final acceptance
- Budget review

Master budget
- Income and expenditure budgets
- Budgeted statement of profit or loss, statement of financial position and cash budget

Preparing functional budgets

- Principle budget factor

Setting up a budget
- Identify the principal budget factor
- Work the budgets around it

Asset vs expense items

- Asset = acquisition of NCA or improvement in earning capacity
- Expense = purpose of trade or to maintain existing earning capacity of NCA

Recording transactions
- Asset = SOFP
- Expense = SOP/L

Preparing asset expenditure budgets
- Long-term plans

Cash budgets

- Detailed statement of cash inflows and outflows
- Indication of expected cash surplus/deficit

Cash management

Cash management

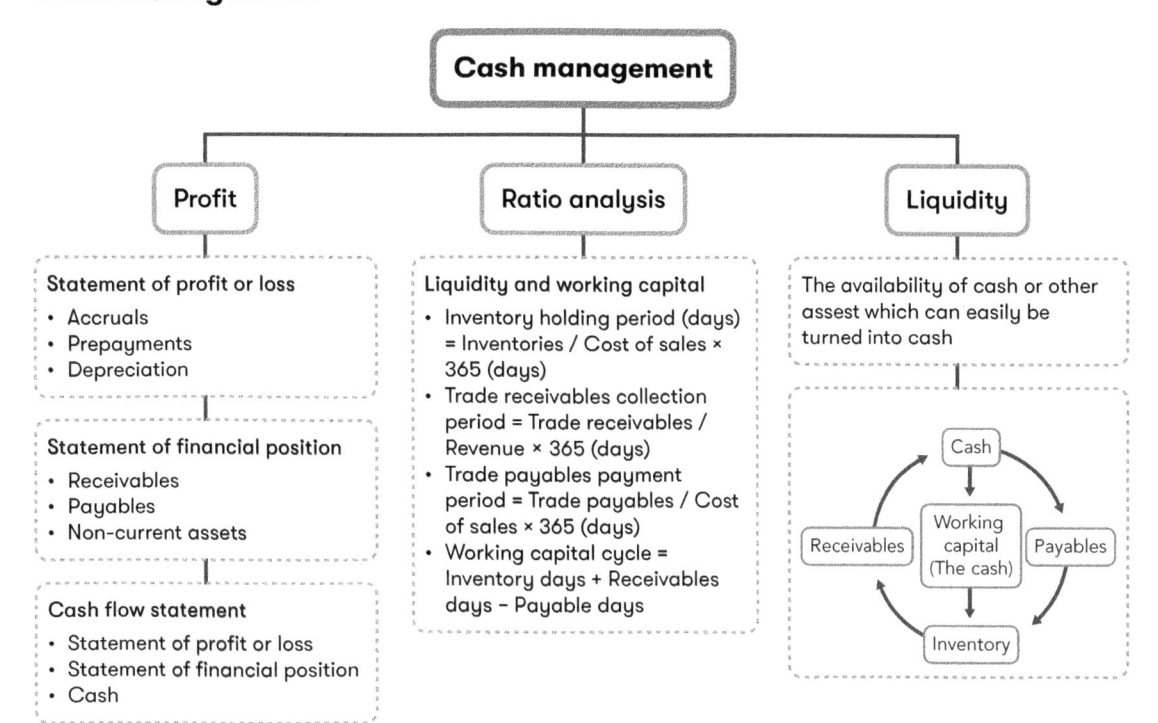

Profit

Statement of profit or loss
- Accruals
- Prepayments
- Depreciation

Statement of financial position
- Receivables
- Payables
- Non-current assets

Cash flow statement
- Statement of profit or loss
- Statement of financial position
- Cash

Ratio analysis

Liquidity and working capital
- Inventory holding period (days) = Inventories / Cost of sales × 365 (days)
- Trade receivables collection period = Trade receivables / Revenue × 365 (days)
- Trade payables payment period = Trade payables / Cost of sales × 365 (days)
- Working capital cycle = Inventory days + Receivables days − Payable days

Liquidity

The availability of cash or other assest which can easily be turned into cash

Working capital cycle: Cash → Payables → Inventory → Receivables → Cash (Working capital (The cash))

MATS Practice Tasks

Task 3.1

(a) Which of the following are purposes of management information? Select all that apply.

	✓
Controlling the organisation	
Meeting legal requirements	
Planning future operations	
Management decision making	

(b) Which of the following is a management planning activity?

	✓
Valuing inventory	
Preparing a budget	
Selecting the most appropriate investment	
Analysing variances	

(c) The total of which of the following costs form a product's prime cost? Select all that apply.

	✓
Direct labour	
Direct material	
Direct expenses	
Production overheads	
Selling and distribution overheads	

Task 3.2

Lothar is paid a basic hourly rate of £20 per hour for a 35-hour week. His hourly rate of pay for any overtime hours is 25% more than his hourly rate. In March, Lothar worked 15 hours overtime.

Required

(a) What is the overtime premium paid to Lothar for March?

£ ☐

Lothar's overtime was for a one-off event which is not attributable to a particular customer order.

Required

(b) Lothar's overtime premium should be treated as a:

	✓
Direct cost	
Indirect cost	

(c) Which of the following is the correct double entry to record direct labour costs?

	✓
DR Wages control CR Production	
DR Wages control CR Production overheads	
DR Production CR Wages control	
DR Production overheads CR Wages control	

(d) In which account are direct material costs recorded?

	✓
Production overhead control account	
Production control account	

(e) Natwich Ltd manufactures small wooden toys. How would it account for consumables needed by its head office laser printers?

	✓
As a production cost	
As a production overhead	
As a non-production cost	
As a non-production overhead	

Kilofish Ltd is a manufacturing company. It has already recorded the following entry in its accounts in respect of a production overhead which has been incurred.

DR Production Overheads £15,000 CR Payables £15,000

Kilofish's management accountant now must record the actual amount of the overhead which has been absorbed in production (£17,500).

Required

(f) Which of the following shows the correct double entry for this transaction?

	✓
DR Production £17,500, CR Production overheads £17,500	
DR Production overheads £17,500, CR Production £17,500	
DR Production £17,500, CR Statement of profit or loss £17,500	
DR Production overheads £17,500, CR Statement of profit or loss £17,500	

(g) Which of the following correctly states the situation regarding Kilofish Ltd and the production overhead that it has recorded?

	✓
The production overhead was over-absorbed	
The production overhead was under-absorbed	
The production overhead was neither over nor under absorbed	

Task 3.3

(a) Which type of cost changes directly in relation to changes in production volume?

	✓
Fixed	
Variable	
Stepped	

(b) A mobile phone bill is an example of which type of cost?

	✓
Fixed	
Variable	
Stepped	
Semi-variable	

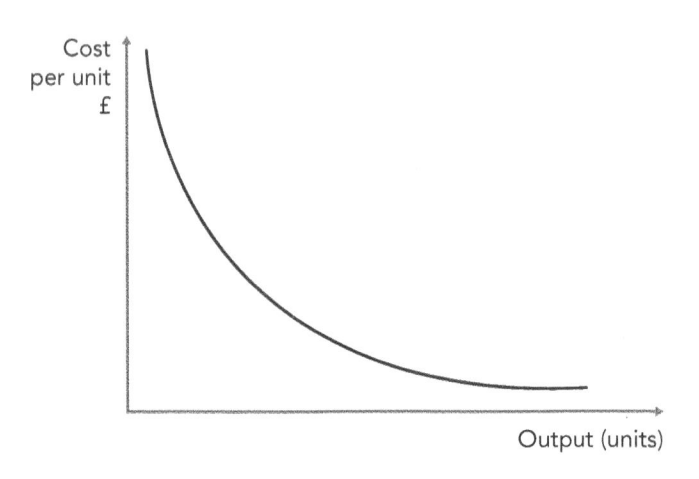

Required

(c) Which type of cost does this graph show?

	✓
Variable	
Stepped	
Fixed	
Semi-variable	

Task 3.4

(a) Which of the following statements regarding job costing is/are correct? Select all that apply.

	✓
There is no price list	
There is no standard product	
Each job will have different costs	
It is often used by service organisations	

(b) Composite cost units are often used by organisations operating which costing system?

	✓
Batch costing	
Job costing	
Service costing	
Process costing	

Luxchem Ltd produces a range of dyes used by clothes manufactures to colour the clothes that they produce. Last week, Luxchem Ltd made a batch of colour DU34. 1,000 litres of a liquid was added to the process and 934 litres was produced by the process. Normal loss is 5%.

Required

(c) Calculate the normal loss for the process.

[ ] litres

(d) In this process there was an:

	✓
Abnormal loss	
Abnormal gain	

Task 3.5

(a) Complete the following statement by selecting the correct options to complete the gaps.

To calculate the direct labour cost for a cost unit, you multiply the [▼] by the [▼].

Picklist
- Labour rate per day
- Labour rate per hour
- Number of labour hours needed to produce one unit
- Total direct labour cost
- Total units produced
- Units produced per day

A business is planning to produce 10,000 units of output in the next budget period. Each unit requires 7 kg of materials and 5% of materials are wasted in the process.

Required

(b) What is the total amount of materials needed in the budget period? Round your answer to the nearest whole number.

[_____] kg

(c) Complete the following statement by selecting the correct option to complete the gap below.

A master budget is an example of a [▼]

Picklist
- Fixed budget
- Flexed budget
- Flexible budget

Joinery Ltd is preparing a budget schedule based on two possible levels of output, 500 units and 750 units.

Direct material costs are £1 per unit.

Factory rates for the budget period at £75,000

Required

(d) Complete the following statements.

Direct material costs for 500 units are £ [_____] and for 750 units are £ [_____]

Factory rates for 500 units are £ [_____] and for 750 units are £ [_____]

(e) With a rolling budget, a set amount of time is always included in the budget.

	✓
True	
False	

Task 3.6

(a) Complete the table to show the materials variance and whether it is adverse or favourable.

	Budgeted (£)	Actual (£)	Variance (£)	Adverse/ Favourable
Materials	220,375	202,578		▼

Picklist
- Adverse
- Favourable

(b) Which of the following are possible causes for an adverse materials variance? Select all that apply.

	✓
Careless purchasing	
Increase in idle time	
Lack of staff training in production teams	
Theft	
Stricter quality control	

(c) Complete the following statement by selecting the correct options to complete the gaps below.

The total variable overhead variance is the difference between the [▼] for the period and the [▼] for the [▼].

Picklist
- Actual cost of variable overhead
- Actual production in the period
- Budgeted cost of variable overhead
- Budgeted production in the period

(d) Complete the following statement by selecting the correct options to complete the gaps below.

The sales price variance is the difference between the [▼] and the [▼] for the [▼].

Picklist
- Actual level of sales
- Actual revenue received
- Budgeted level of sales
- Budgeted revenue received

Task 3.7

Larch Ltd is preparing a cash budget based on the following budgeted sales:

January £175,500

February £225,575

March £202,654

All sales are on credit. 80% of receipts come in one month after the sale and the rest comes in two months after the sale.

Required

(a) Calculate Larch Ltd's budgeted cash receipts for March.

£ [ ]

(b) Which of the following is a manager of a profit centre responsible for? Select all that apply.

	✓
Costs	
Profits	
Investments	

(c) Complete the following statement by selecting the correct option to complete the gap below.

The [▼] limits an organisation's performance for a given period and is often the starting point in budget preparation.

Picklist
- Master budget
- Principal budget factor

(d) Complete the following statement by selecting the correct option to complete the gap below.

It is important for the motivation of responsibility centre managers that they are only accountable for [▼].

Picklist
- Avoidable costs
- Budgeted costs
- Controllable costs
- Sunk costs

(e) When budgeting for asset expenditure, the statement of profit or loss can be ignored.

	✓
True	
False	

(f) When budgeting for income, money the business receives from investments, such as dividend income, should be budgeted as capital income.

	✓
True	
False	

Task 3.8

(a) Identify whether the following relate to cash or non-cash items.

	Cash item ✓	Non-cash item ✓
Accruals concept		
Owner's capital received		
Provisions for future expenses		
Sale of office equipment		

(b) Which of the following assets is the LEAST liquid?

	✓
Shares purchased from the stock exchange	
Cash held in fixed term investments	
Trade receivables	
Cash at bank	

The following extracts have been taken from a company's financial statements:

Inventory: £3,766

Cost of sales: £10,575

Required

(c) Calculate the company's inventory holding period. Round your answer to the nearest whole number.

[ ] days

The following liquidity ratios are available for Murcio Ltd.

Trade receivables days: 37 days

Trade payables days: 40 days

Inventory holding period: 60 days

Required

(d) Calculate Murcio Ltd's working capital cycle.

[ ] days

(e) Which of the following actions would help a business REDUCE its working capital cycle?

	✓
Chase late-paying customers	
Pay suppliers earlier	
Sell non-current assets	
Increase inventory levels	

Chapter 4 – Business Awareness (BUAW)

BUAW Summaries

The diagrams that follow are summaries from 'Business Awareness (BUAW)' covering the key areas most relevant to your EPA Knowledge assessment. The summaries and tasks included in this chapter are based on the AAT 'Scope of content – knowledge assessment' mapping contained in the AAT End Point Assessment Specification.

Stakeholders

Stakeholders
└── **What are stakeholders?**

Classifications of stakeholders
- Internal:
  - Corporate management
  - Employees
- Connected:
  - Shareholders
  - Debt holders (eg bank)
  - Intermediate (business) and final (consumer) customers
  - Suppliers
- External:
  - Immediate community/society at large
  - Competitors
  - Special interest groups
  - Government

Stakeholder management
- Mendelow's matrix

Sustainability

Sustainability
├── **What is sustainability?**
└── **Challenges of sustainability**

What is sustainability?
- Social justice
- Environmental quality
- Economic prosperity

Challenges of sustainability
- Long-term vs short-term views
- Stakeholder views
- Resource management
- Holistic impact
- Accountants - 'public interest' duty

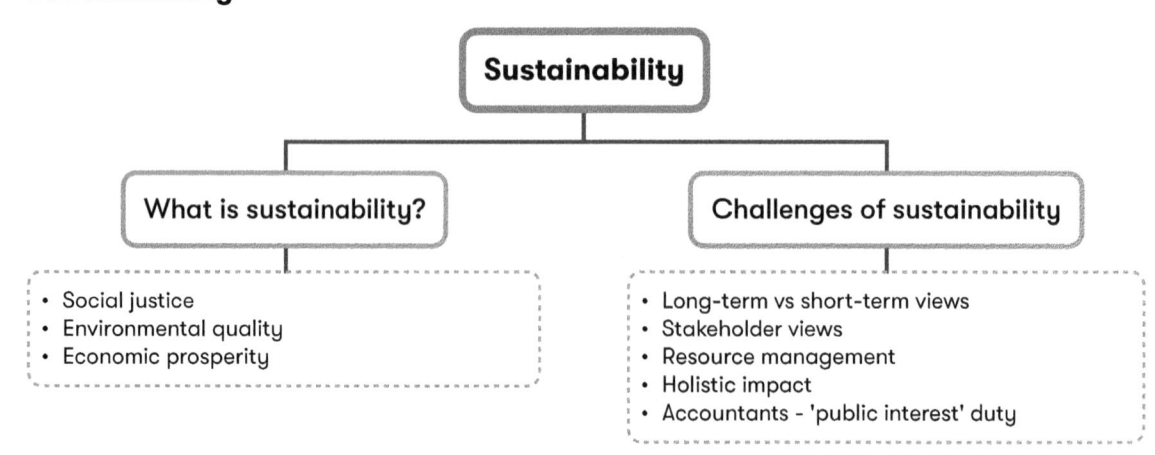

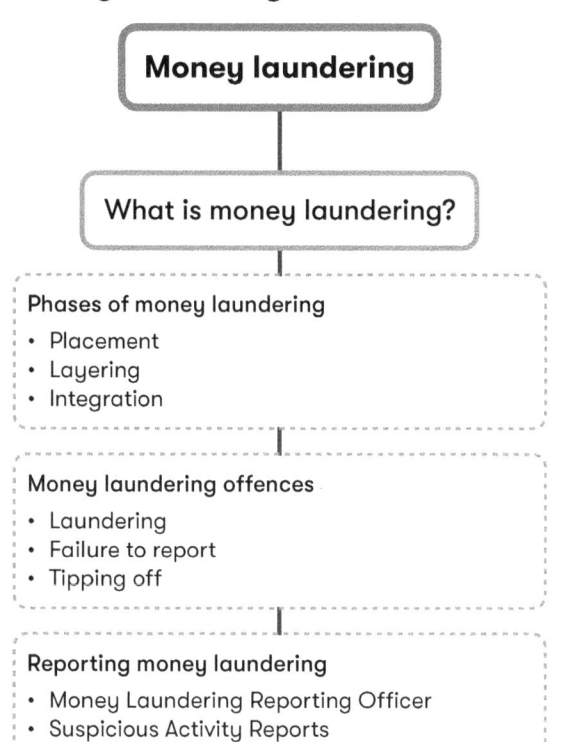

Professional ethics for accountants

Professional ethics for accountants
- AAT's Code of Ethics
  - Objectivity
  - Professional competence
  - Professional behaviour
    - Threats
    - Safeguards
  - Integrity
  - Confidentiality

Money laundering

Money laundering
- What is money laundering?

Phases of money laundering
- Placement
- Layering
- Integration

Money laundering offences
- Laundering
- Failure to report
- Tipping off

Reporting money laundering
- Money Laundering Reporting Officer
- Suspicious Activity Reports

Technology and data

Technology and data
└── **IT in Accounting**
- Information
- Process automation
- Data protection
  - Seven principles
  - Processing data
  - Cyber risks
  - Cyber security
- Outsourcing and offshoring
- New technologies
  - Blockchain
  - AI
  - Big data
  - Cloud

Communicating data

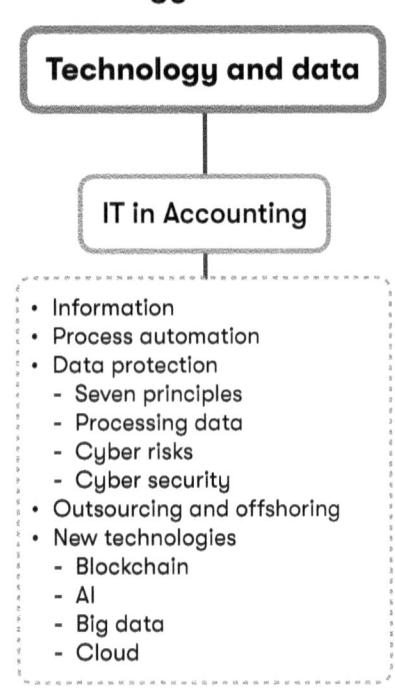

Communicating data
├── **Communication**
- Process
- Professional communication

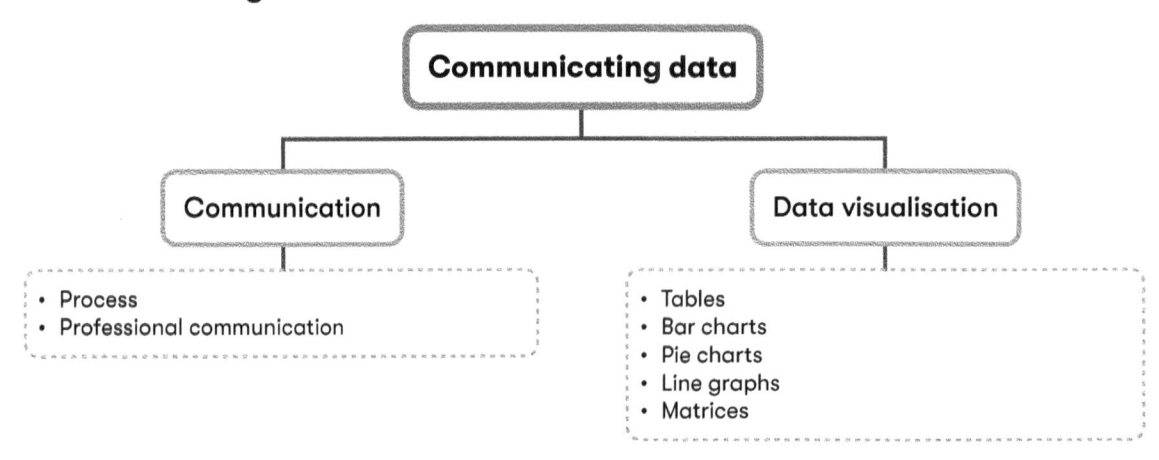

└── **Data visualisation**
- Tables
- Bar charts
- Pie charts
- Line graphs
- Matrices

BUAW Practice Tasks

Task 4.1

(a) Categorise the following stakeholders as internal, connected or external.

Stakeholder	Internal ✓	Connected ✓	External ✓
Shareholders			
Suppliers			
Directors			
Competitors			

(b) Identify whether the following statements regarding Mendelow's matrix are true or false.

Statement	True ✓	False ✓
Mendelow's matrix helps an organisation to assess each stakeholder's likely reaction to a business decision		
Mendelow's matrix helps an organisation to evaluate actions that may ease the acceptance of a business decision		

(c) According to Mendelow's matrix, which of the following stakeholders should an organisation 'keep satisfied'?

	✓
Agatha, who has low interest and low power in the organisation	
Bjorn, who has high interest and low power in the organisation	
Cynthia, who has high power and low interest in the organisation	
Drake, who has high power and high interest in the organisation	

Task 4.2

(a) Identify whether the following statements regarding sustainability are true or false.

Statement	True ✓	False ✓
Sustainability is only a concern of the special interest groups of an organisation's stakeholders		
Sustainability requires organisations to carefully consider how they manage resources		
Sustainability requires a company to take a holistic view		
Sustainability requires companies to adopt a short-term view of profits		

(b) Match the following business activities with the associated sustainability terms.

Business activity	Social justice ✓	Environmental quality ✓	Economic prosperity ✓
Offsetting carbon emissions			
Being a good corporate citizen			
Paying a fair share of tax			

Task 4.3

Rajesh is a part qualified accounting technician who has recently become employed by RMS Accountancy, a medium sized firm which provides a variety of bookkeeping and accounting services for local businesses.

Rajesh and Jennifer, another accountant at RMS, have been discussing professional ethics and the ways in which the AAT Code of Professional Ethics applies to them. During this discussion Rajesh made the following comments.

Required

(a) Identify whether the following statements are true or false.

	True ✓	False ✓
'I know I act ethically as I have never broken the law and always comply with regulations.'		
'The AAT Code of Professional Ethics is legally binding if you are a member of the AAT.'		

One of RMS's clients, Carmichael Ltd, has been allocated to Rajesh. Carmichael Ltd is owned by Rajesh's sister, Manju.

Required

(b) This situation represents which one of the following threats to Rajesh's compliance with the fundamental principles?

	✓
Familiarity	
Self-interest	
Advocacy	

(c) If Rajesh carries out this work, which fundamental principle would he be most at risk of breaching?

	✓
Integrity	
Objectivity	
Confidentiality	

(d) Which is the most appropriate action for Rajesh to take?

	✓
Resign from RMS Accountancy	
Inform RMS Accountancy of his link with Carmichael Ltd	
Inform the AAT of his link with Carmichael Ltd	

RMS Accountancy prides itself on its strong ethical culture which can, in part, be attributed to the 'tone-at-the-top'.

Required

(e) Which of the below statements best describes what is meant by the tone-at-the-top?

	✓
Leaders of the firm have issued clear policies on the ethical behaviour expected at RMS Accountancy.	
Leaders of the firm demonstrate the importance of compliance with the fundamental principles.	
Leaders of the firm require that any potential threat to the fundamental principles is communicated to them in order for the most appropriate action to be taken.	

(f) Identify whether the following statements are true or false.

Statement	True ✓	False ✓
'The AAT Code of Professional Ethics does not apply to me yet as I am only a student accounting technician.'		
'Ethical codes provide advice as to how to comply with the law.'		

(g) Complete the following sentence by filling in the blank.

If you have an ethical concern at work, usually the most appropriate first course of action would be to raise this with [▼].

Picklist
- A trusted colleague
- An employee helpline
- The AAT

(h) In which of the following situations would an accountant be required to breach confidentiality? Select all that apply.

	✓
Providing working papers to a new firm who is taking on a former client	
As a result of an enquiry by AAT	
To a financial institution who has requested the information directly from your firm of accountants	
To protect a member's professional interest in a court of law	

Task 4.4

(a) Which of the following is the first stage in the money laundering process?

	✓
Layering	
Placement	
Integration	

Rita has discovered that she may have been involved in a money laundering operation without her knowledge. She is worried that she may be incriminated if she reports the issue and is fearful of losing her job and damaging her reputation. The money laundering scheme was very small scale and so Rita makes the decision not to disclose the matter. She confronts the perpetrator and informs them that she will have no further dealings with them.

Required

(b) Could Rita be guilty of money laundering?

	✓
No, she was unaware of being involved in money laundering and withdrew from the engagement as soon as she suspected wrong doing.	
No, the money laundering scheme was very small scale and would therefore be below the threshold for criminal conviction.	
Yes, if she has been part of the scheme, even unknowingly, she could still be guilty of money laundering.	

(c) Show whether the below statements are true or false.

Statement	True ✓	False ✓
Rita has tipped off the client.		
If Rita does fail to disclose her suspicions of money laundering she may face additional charges.		

Rita's colleague, Alfred, is another accountant working her practice. He has begun to suspect one of his clients, François, of money laundering.

Required

(d) Select which of the following statements are true or false.

Statement	True ✓	False ✓
Alfred is required to report his suspicions to the AAT		
Failure to disclose money laundering suspicions can result in imprisonment		
Alfred must ensure that he makes François aware that the relevant disclosures have been made.		

Task 4.5

(a) Select from the following technologies to complete the sentence below.

[▼] is one form of distributed ledger technology.

Picklist
- Artificial intelligence
- Big data
- Blockchain
- Cloud computing
- Process automation

"Big data is often unstructured and can take many forms including free text, images, and audio."

Required

(b) Which characteristic of big data does this statement describe?

	✓
Value	
Veracity	
Variety	
Volume	
Velocity	

Data analytics is the collection, management and analysis of large data sets with the objective of discovering useful information that an organisation can use for decision making.

Required

(c) Which of the following technologies could speed up the process of data analytics?

	✓
Blockchain	
Robotic process automation	
Artificial intelligence	
Cloud accounting	

(d) Complete the following sentence by filling in the blanks.

When a service provider uses [▼] resources to create their [▼], the result is called [▼].

Picklist
- A virtual private cloud
- Cloud computing
- Private cloud
- Public cloud

(e) Which of the following are characteristics of cloud computing? Select all that apply.

	✓
Fully managed	
On-demand and self-service	
Sold on demand	
Elastic	

Greenhub Ltd collects data from its customers' social media posts. Its customers include individuals such as Keisha and companies such as Tiltwood plc. Rita works for Greenhub Ltd in the data management team and a key role of hers is to process customer data in accordance with Greenhub Ltd's data processing policy.

Required

(f) Complete the following statements using the options supplied in the list below.

[▼] is a data processor.

[▼] is a data controller.

Keisha [▼] a data subject

Tiltwood plc [▼] a data subject

Picklist
- Greenhub Ltd
- Is
- Is not
- Rita

(g) Identify whether the following are correct descriptions of data protection principles.

Description	Correct ✓	Incorrect ✓
The principle of purpose limitation means that organisations are limited to using data in accordance with their vision, mission and corporate objectives.		
The principle of storage limitation means that organisations can only store that data in government approved systems.		
The principle of data minimisation means that data held by organisations must be adequate, relevant and not excessive.		
The principle of lawfulness, fairness, and transparency means that there must be valid grounds for holding the data.		

(h) Match the description to the cyber security threat.

Description	Distributed denial of service attack (DDoS) ✓	Ransomware ✓
Bots are instructed to overwhelm the organisation's website with a wave of internet traffic so that the system is unable to handle it and may crash		
The cyber-attacker gains access to the user's system to lock their files and prevent access to them.		

(i) Complete the sentence by selecting the correct option.

[▼] is a form of cyber security which involves updating software with uploads to fix security issues.

Picklist
- Access control
- Boundary firewall
- Malware protection
- Patch management

Task 4.6

(a) Identify whether the following characteristics of information relate to the strategic or operational levels in an organisation.

Characteristic	Strategic level ✓	Operational level ✓
Unstructured		
Mainly internally sourced		
Short-term focus		

"Information reflects the needs of the user."

Required

(b) Which characteristic of good quality information does the statement describe?

	✓
Understandable	
Easy to use	
Relevant	
Accurate	

Polly is creating a business communication to send to Ralph. Her communication is tailored to her specific purpose and she is conscious of meeting the information needs, language and capabilities of Ralph.

Required

(c) Which attribute of appropriate communication is Polly demonstrating?

	✓
Technically correct	
Achieving its purpose	
Clearly understandable	
Professionally presented	

(d) Data visualisation is an important tool for ensuring printed reports are easy to read.

	✓
True	
False	

(e) Identify which of the following are aspects of data visualisation tools that users should be aware of. Select all that apply.

	✓
Information must be generated as close to the time it is needed for decision making.	
Patterns and anomalies in the data are easy to spot	
Information can be drilled into	
Data visualisation supports efficient decision making	

(f) Match the description to the method of communication.

Description	Bar chart ✓	Line graph ✓
Useful for showing or comparing magnitudes or sizes of items		
Useful for showing the relationship between two variables		

(g) Complete the sentence using the available options.

[▼] show the relationship between items.

Picklist
- Matrix diagrams
- Pie charts
- Tables

Answers

Chapter 1 – Tax Processes for Business (TPFB)

Task 1.1

(a) The correct answers are:

	True ✓	False ✓
Notes To Go may reclaim VAT on its purchases through its VAT returns.	✓	
The VAT on Notes To Go's purchases is known as output tax.		✓

(b) The correct answers are:

	✓
Stationary net cost £100	✓
Stationary net cost £120	
Postage stamps net cost £120	✓
Postage stamps net cost £100	

(c) The correct answers are:

	True ✓	False ✓
Notes To Go is making exempt supplies.		✓
The amount of VAT on any sale of printed music will be zero.	✓	

(d) The correct answers are:

	✓
Registration may improve the image of the business.	✓
VAT returns need to be prepared on a regular basis.	
VAT on Notes To Go's purchases may be reclaimed.	✓

(e) Turnover last year was [above] the VAT registration threshold.

Notes To Go could apply to HMRC to deregister [because supplies are zero-rated].

If Notes To Go deregistered, issuing VAT receipts in the future would be [prohibited].

(f) Your employer's electricity bill is [£175] net of VAT.

Your home electricity bill is [£200] net of VAT.

The VAT on your home electricity bill is borne by [yourself].

Task 1.2

(a) VAT is initially collected by [traders].

VAT is eventually borne by [the final consumer].

(b) VAT is an indirect tax because it is based on [transactions].

The sweets sold by Harpreet are [goods].

(c) The correct answers are:

	True ✓	False ✓
We only need to charge VAT if our customers are also VAT registered.		✓
We do not need to charge VAT if our customers pay in cash.		✓

(d) The correct answer is:

	✓
The VAT fraction can be used to find the VAT from the gross sales price.	✓
The VAT fraction for reduced-rated supplies is 5%.	

(e) Sweets: £ [150]

£180 × 5/6 = £150

(f) Children's colouring books £ [180]

The books are zero rated so there is no VAT to deduct to arrive at the net cost. The net cost is therefore £180.

(g) VAT returns are usually made for [three months].

The deadline for submission is [one month] and [seven days] after the three-month VAT return period.

The deadline for BACS or CHAPS payment is [the same as for the return].

VAT direct debits are taken [three] [working days] after the normal payment deadline.

Task 1.3

(a) **Attributable to taxable supplies**

	£
Directly allocated	5,000
Indirectly allocated:	
3,000 × 25,000/28,200 (89%)	2,670
Total taxable inputs	7,670

Attributable to exempt supplies

	£
Directly allocated	1,100
Indirectly allocated:	
(3,000 – 2,670)	330
Total exempt inputs	1,430

Taxable supplies/Total supplies = 25,000/28,200 = 88.65% = 89% rounded up to next whole %

(b) The total of the exempt input VAT is only recoverable if it is below the de minimis limit:

The amount is below £625 per month on average, and it is ≤ 50% of the total input tax for the period.

(c) Input VAT to recover is £ 9,100

Total exempt input VAT £1,430/3 = £477 which is < £625 per month on average.

£1,430/£9,100 × 100% = 15.7% meaning exempt input VAT is < 50% of total input VAT.

As both parts of the de minimis test are met, Camden Ltd can recover all of its input VAT of £9,100.

(d) The correct answers are:

	✓
Output VAT of 20% will be charged on the sale, and this can be recovered as input VAT on the next VAT return.	
Goods sold to overseas customers are referred to as exports.	✓
Exports are always zero rated, provided the trader obtains evidence of their export within three months.	✓
Exports are always exempt, provided the trader obtains evidence of their export within three months.	

(e) Goods which are purchased from overseas countries are known as imports .

[No VAT] is charged by the supplier. When the goods enter the UK, the [purchaser] needs to pay the applicable rate of UK VAT.

Task 1.4

(a) The correct answer is:

	✓
£20 spent at a toll bridge while travelling.	
Goods costing £35 bought from a vending machine.	✓

Tutorial note. An invoice is not needed for the £20 spent at a toll bridge because the expenditure total is £25 or less including VAT, so no invoice is required to reclaim VAT, a simple receipt is acceptable.

(b) All records [may] be kept digitally, and certain records [must] be kept digitally under 'Making Tax Digital' rules.

All records are to be kept for at least [six] years.

Tutorial note. All records may be kept digitally, and certain records must be kept digitally under the 'Making Tax Digital' rules. Under MTD these include:
- The business name, address and VAT registration number
- The VAT on goods and services both supplied and received
- The time of supply and value of supply of all sales and purchases
- The rate of VAT applied to all sales made

(c) Amount of VAT £ [66.33]

(d) Amount of VAT £ [0]

(e) The correct answer is:

	✓
The debt must be more than six years overdue.	
The input tax must have been paid by the client.	
The output tax must have been paid to HMRC.	✓

(f) The correct answers are:

	True ✓	False ✓
Relief is claimed through the VAT return as a deduction from output tax.		✓

Tutorial note. The VAT being reclaimed on the bad debt is recorded as input VAT, rather than a reduction in output VAT.

(g) Bad debts expense account is [debited] with [£1,000].

The VAT account is [debited] with [£200].

The sales ledger control account is [credited] with [£1,200].

Task 1.5

(a) Debbie would like to offer a 5% discount to Bizyness Ltd if they buy 20 or more doors in a single order.

If Bizyness Ltd goes ahead and orders 20 doors at one time, the discount would be a [trade] discount.

(b) Debbie would like to offer a 5% discount to Harold if he buys a back door and pays within 14 days of this being fitted.

The discount offered would be a [prompt payment] or [settlement] discount.

(c) The correct answers are:

	✓
The deadline for payment for the discount to apply.	✓
The amount of the discount.	✓
The VAT on the discounted price.	✓
A statement that no credit note will be issued.	

(d) The actual tax point is [20 April 20X8].

> **Tutorial note.** The invoice is issued within 14 days after the basic tax point and so becomes the actual tax point.

(e) The tax point for the deposit of £500 is [16 January 20X9].

The tax point for the balance of £700 is [30 January 20X9].

> **Tutorial note. Tax point for the deposit** – The deposit payment is the earliest date (ignoring the order date). The tax point for a deposit is determined by looking at the earliest of:
>
> The basic tax point (despatch date) – 30th January
>
> The invoice date – 18th February
>
> The deposit payment date – 16th January
>
> **Tax point for the balancing payment** – The earliest of:
>
> The basic tax point (despatch date) – 30th January
>
> The invoice date – 18th February
>
> The date of payment for the balance – 23rd February

Task 1.6

(a)

	Paid in 7 days time £	Paid in 14 days time £	Paid in 20 days time £
Net value	2,400	2,400	2,400
Discount %	10%	5%	0%
Discounted net value	2,160	2,280	2,400
VAT on standard rated goods	432	456	480
Gross amount payable by the customer	2,592	2,736	2,880

(b) The correct answer is:

	✓
More VAT payable	
Less VAT payable	✓

The credit note will decrease the output tax, and so less VAT will be payable.

(c) The correct answer is:

	✓
Issue a credit note for £50 including VAT	
Take no action	
Issue a further invoice for £50 plus VAT	
Issue a credit note for £50 plus VAT	✓

(d) Debbie can issue an invoice for the [full amount], followed by a [credit note] if the discount [is taken up].

or

Debbie can issue [one invoice], with [both] possible prices and VAT amounts specified, with clear instructions to the customer regarding recoverability of their input VAT.

(e) The correct answers are:

	✓
Sales daybook	✓
Purchases daybook	
Cash receipts book	✓
Cash payments book	

Task 1.7

(a) The correct answers are:

	✓
A sequential invoice number	✓
The time of the supply	✓
Details of the deadline for payment	
The date of issue of the document (where different to the time of supply)	✓
Kaykes' address	✓
Kaykes' VAT registration number as supplier	✓
The date from which Kaykes was registered for VAT	
A brief description of the type(s) of cake	✓
The number of each type of cake bought	✓
Sate Ltd's address	✓
Sate Ltd's Company registration number	
Sate Ltd's VAT registration number	
A £ sign to show the currency	✓
The rate of VAT	✓
The total amount of VAT chargeable	✓

Tutorial note. Contents of a Full VAT invoice (AAT TPFB Reference Material)

- A sequential number based on one or more series which uniquely identifies the document
- The time of the supply (tax point)
- The date of issue of the document (where different to the time of supply)
- Supplier's name, address and VAT registration number
- Customer's name and address
- A description sufficient to identify the goods or services supplied
- For each description, the quantity of the goods or the extent of the services, the rate of VAT, and the amount payable excluding VAT – this can be expressed in any currency
- The gross total amount payable, excluding VAT – this can be expressed in any currency
- The rate of any cash discount offered
- The total amount of VAT chargeable – this must be expressed in sterling
- The unit price (applicable to countable elements)

(b) The correct answers are:

	✓
VAT-registered businesses must raise a VAT invoice (paper or electronic) when they make a taxable supply to another VAT-registered business.	✓
A taxable person can always reclaim input VAT.	
If the customer is not VAT-registered, a VAT invoice is still mandatory.	
A VAT invoice must be raised within 30 days of the supply.	✓

Tutorial note. A taxable person can only reclaim input VAT if they have a valid VAT invoice for the purchase.

If the customer is not VAT-registered, then a VAT invoice is not mandatory, unless requested by the customer.

(c) The correct answers are:

	✓
Kaykes will need to implement procedures to ensure the authenticity and integrity of their electronic invoices.	✓
Kaykes' customers must settle the invoices via bank transfer.	
Kaykes' customers must agree to receive electronic invoices.	✓
The file type must enable invoices to be amended (eg Word document).	
HMRC must receive copies of all electronic invoices issued.	

(d) For supplies invoiced at [less] than £250, including VAT, a business may issue a less detailed [simplified] invoice.

If [retail supplies] are sold for [more] than £250, a [modified] invoice may be issued.

Task 1.8

(a) The amount of VAT due is £ [2,475]

£20,000 × 1.2 = £24,000 + £9,000 = £33,000

£33,000 × 7.5% = £2,475

No input VAT can be reclaimed on the purchases of components or services under the FRS.

The charity donation is outside the scope of VAT.

(b) The VAT payable to HMRC calculated above is shown in [box 1] of the VAT return.

The figure shown in box 6 will be [£33,000] which is the total VAT- [inclusive] sales.

Tutorial note. The flat rate scheme makes the calculation of the VAT liability simpler, by calculating the amount of VAT payable as a flat (generally industry-specific) percentage of total VAT-inclusive turnover (including exempt turnover).

(c) A business can apply to register for the flat rate scheme provided that VAT-exclusive taxable turnover is not expected to exceed £150,000 in the next 12 months.

> **Tutorial note.** To join the scheme VAT-exclusive taxable turnover should not be expected to exceed £150,000 in the next 12 months.
>
> A business must leave the scheme if VAT-inclusive total supplies (including exempt supplies) exceed £230,000 in the previous 12 months (or are expected to exceed this in the following 12 months).

(d) The correct answers are:

	✓
Output VAT is not paid until it has been collected from the customer, giving a cash flow advantage.	
Cashflow can be managed as the VAT is payable based on a percentage of turnover.	✓
Only one VAT return needs to be submitted.	
VAT payable is normally less than the amount payable under the standard accounting scheme.	✓
A business can choose which flat rate percentage it wants to use in order to calculate the lowest VAT liability.	
There will be simplified administration as VAT does not have to be accounted for on each individual sales or purchase invoice.	✓
A business using the flat rate scheme can always claim back input VAT on larger fixed assets.	

> **Tutorial note.** If a flat-rate trader incurs input VAT on the acquisition of larger fixed assets (those with a VAT inclusive cost over £2,000), this can be reclaimed via the VAT return. Smaller fixed asset purchases are reflected in the flat rate percentage.

(e) The correct answers are:

	True ✓	False ✓
Businesses using the flat rate scheme can also use the cash accounting scheme.		✓
The scheme can only be used when a business's VAT-exclusive taxable turnover is not expected to exceed £1,350,000 in the next 12 months.	✓	
A business must leave the cash accounting scheme if VAT-exclusive taxable supplies exceed £1,600,000 in the previous 12 months.	✓	
The cash accounting scheme enables businesses to ignore the tax point rules and account for VAT only when it is paid and received.	✓	

Task 1.9

(a)

	£	£
Output VAT		
£201,000 x 20%		40,200
Input VAT		
Wages	0	
Stationary £2,760/6	460	
Computer £1,800/6	300	
Travel	0	
Car	0	
Charity	0	
Total input VAT to deduct		(760)
VAT payable		39,440

(b) Nine payments on account must be made.

Each payment is 10% of the previous years' VAT liability, being £4,000 each.

Tutorial note. The previous year's liability was £36,000.

£36,000/9 = £4,000 each POA.

(c) The first payment is due in April and then every month until December.

Any balance is due two months after the VAT year end, along with the VAT return.

(d) The correct answers are:

	✓
VAT-exclusive taxable turnover is not expected to exceed £1,350,000 in the next 12 months.	✓
VAT-inclusive taxable turnover is not expected to exceed £1,350,000 in the next 12 months.	
If VAT-exclusive taxable supplies exceed £1,600,000 at the end of the VAT accounting year, the business must leave the scheme.	✓
If VAT-inclusive taxable supplies exceed £1,600,000 at the end of the VAT accounting year, the business must leave the scheme.	

Tutorial note. It is the VAT-exclusive figures used for joining and leaving the scheme, not the VAT-inclusive figures.

(e) The correct answers are:

	✓
Submitting only one VAT return reduces the administrative burden of VAT.	
If turnover decreases, the interim payments may be higher than they need to be.	✓
The business will have to wait until the end of the year when it submits its return for a refund.	✓
The business has an extra month between the end of the VAT period and the return submission date.	

(f) A trader may alternatively opt for three , quarterly payments of 25% of the previous year's VAT liability.

These payments are due at the end of months 4 , 7 and 10 in the VAT year.

The balance is due with the return as for traders who make nine, monthly payments.

Task 1.10

(a) The correct answers are:

	✓
Once installed, payroll software will never need to be updated.	
Payroll software is used to provide information to HMRC under Real Time Information (RTI).	✓
Payroll software can calculate statutory maternity pay.	✓
All payroll software that is tested and approved by HRMC will be suitable for any business.	

(b)

Form	Function
Full Payment Submission (FPS)	Return showing pay and deductions for each employee on a specific payment date
P11D	End of year summary of taxable benefits
P45	Details of employee leaving
P60	End of year summary of pay and deductions

(c) A Full Payment Submission (FPS) form must be filed with HMRC every time employees are paid .

An Employer Payment Summary (EPS) must be filed every month where no employees are paid.

(d) The correct answers are:

	True ✓	False ✓
A maximum penalty of £3,000 per year may apply for failure to maintain full records.	✓	
HMRC may make an unannounced visit to an employer's premises to inspect payroll records.		✓
HMRC do not require employers to keep records of Payroll Giving Scheme documents.		✓
Records are required to be maintained for three years from the end of the relevant tax year to which they relate.	✓	

(e) The form P60 | must | be provided to each employee by | 31 May | following the end of the | tax year |.

A copy of the form P11D | must | be provided to the employee by | 6 July | following the end of the | tax year |.

A PAYE settlement agreement (PSA) is where the employer agrees to pay the employees' income tax on | any minor or irregular benefits |.

Task 1.11

(a)

	£
Output VAT overstated by	(400.00)
Input VAT overstated by	63.00
Net error	(337.00)

Tutorial note. Input VAT is overstated by £70 – £7 = £63.00

Output VAT overstated by £400.00

Net error is overstatement of output VAT of £337.00

(b) The correct answer is:

	✓
A correction cannot be made on the next return as the error exceeds £10,000.	
A correction can be made on the next VAT return as the error is less than 1% of turnover.	
A correction cannot be made on the next return as the error exceeds £50,000.	✓

> **Tutorial note.** The error is less than 1% of turnover, but that is subject to an overall limit of £50,000.

(c) The error correction threshold is the greater of:

£ 10,000 and 1 % of turnover, subject to an overall limit of £ 50,000 .

(d) The correct answer is:

	✓
It shouldn't be shown on the VAT return.	
It should be shown in box 1 of the VAT return.	
It should be shown in box 4 of the VAT return.	✓

> **Tutorial note.** It is shown as an increase in the input tax at box 4 on the VAT return.

(e) The correct answers are:

	✓
If a VAT return is submitted late and there is no VAT due, there will be no penalty implications.	
Each time a taxpayer submits a VAT return late, this counts as a failure and each failure gets one penalty point.	✓
There is no financial penalty until the taxpayer reaches the penalty point threshold.	✓
Individual penalty points expire after one year.	

> **Tutorial note.** If a return is submitted late, even if no VAT is due, this will still give rise to a penalty point.
>
> Individual penalty points expire two years from the end of the month of the failure.

(f) The correct answers are:

	True ✓	False ✓
If the VAT is paid late to HMRC, then no penalty is payable if the liability is settled within 15 days.	✓	
If the VAT is outstanding after 15 days a penalty is charged at HMRC's discretion.		✓
If the VAT is outstanding after 15 days a penalty of 2% is charged on the amount outstanding.	✓	
If the VAT is outstanding at the end of 30 days, a further 4% is charged per day.		✓
If the VAT is outstanding at the end of 30 days, a further 2% is charged, and from day 31 onwards 4% per annum is charged.	✓	

> **Tutorial note. Late payment penalty**
>
> If the VAT is paid late to HMRC, then no penalty is payable as long as the liability is settled within 15 days of the due date or a time to pay arrangements has been agreed with HMRC.
>
> If the VAT is outstanding after 15 days a penalty is charged. This will be 2% of the amount outstanding at the end of day 15.
>
> A further 2% is charged at the end of day 30 if the VAT is still outstanding.
>
> 4% per annum is charged on unpaid VAT from day 31 onwards, calculated on a daily basis.

(g) If a FPS is late, a penalty of between £ 100 and £ 400 per month is imposed, depending on the number of employees the business has.

> **Tutorial note.** If a FPS is late, insufficient FPSs are filed or an EPS is not filed, a penalty of between £100 and £400 is imposed per month, depending on the number of employees a business has.

Chapter 2 – Financial Accounting: Preparing Financial Statements (FAPS)

Task 2.1

Accounting concept	Description
A transaction should only be included in the final accounts if it can be measured in monetary terms.	Money measurement
Applying the same methods to account for the same or similar items, from period to period within a reporting entity which helps to ensure that information is comparable over time.	Consistency
The exercise of caution when making judgements so that assets, income and profits are not overstated and liabilities, expenses and losses are not understated.	Prudence

Task 2.2

Accounting concept	Description
Income and expenses shown in the statement of profit or loss are those that were earned or incurred during the period rather than the cash received or paid in the period.	Accrual accounting
Omitting, misstating or obscuring information that could reasonably be expected to influence the decisions made by the primary users.	Materiality
The financial statements are normally prepared on the assumption that an entity will continue in operation for the foreseeable future.	Going concern

Task 2.3

Confirmatory value and predictive value enable financial information to be relevant in making a difference to the decisions made by users.

Task 2.4

The correct answers are:

	✓
Your manager asks to review your year-end accounting work in relation to the client (or company).	✓
Another client (or company) asks for details because they want to approach the client (or company) about purchasing their business.	
The client's bank requests to see the financial statements and your client has granted permission.	✓
A friend wants details on the financial situation of your client (or company) because they are considering purchasing shares in the client (company).	

Under the AAT Code of Professional Ethics, you should respect the confidentiality of information acquired as a result of professional and business relationships. It should only be shared with authorised accounting colleagues or with client (or company) permission.

Task 2.5

General ledger account	Financial statement classification
Cost of intangible assets	Non-current assets
Bank overdraft	Current liabilities
Long term bank loan account	Non-current liabilities
Inventory	Current assets
Sales	Income

Task 2.6

Invoices received from suppliers	Purchases daybook
Invoices issued to customers	Sales daybook
Credit notes received from suppliers	Purchases returns daybook
Credit notes issued to customers	Sales returns daybook

The books of prime entry are the records in which transactions are initially recorded. Postings of totals will then be made from the books of prime entry to the ledgers.

Task 2.7

(a) The correct answer is:

	✓
True	✓
False	

VAT may be payable to HMRC or recoverable from HMRC.

(b) The correct answer is:

	✓
True	✓
False	

They contain the same information that is in the memorandum (subsidiary) receivables and payables ledgers; however, they show the totals rather than the individual transactions.

(c) The correct answer is:

	✓
True	
False	✓

Subsidiary ledger accounts are prepared so that the business can see the amount owed from credit customers or to credit suppliers at a point in time. They are additional to and separate from the control accounts that form part of the general ledger.

(d) The correct answer is:

	✓
True	
False	✓

This is like any other control account and helps to ensure that the double entry is made correctly. All payroll liabilities are initially credited to this control account. They are subsequently transferred to the relevant general ledger account (such as HMRC, pension and bank). At the end of a period, once all the necessary payroll entries have been made, this account will have a balance of zero.

The wages expense will be reflected in a separate wages expense general ledger account.

Task 2.8

The correct answers are:

	✓
Accounting software will often automatically transfer data or totals to control accounts based on individual entries made throughout the period.	✓
If accounting software is used to automate a process, then there is no need to review or check the results.	
It is not possible to automate any processes associated with non-current assets.	
Accounting packages can automate the process of updating the control accounts and subsidiary ledgers at the same time to minimise the probability of any differences arising.	✓

Logical, repeatable processes are often automated if accounting packages are used. This will include the calculation and potentially the journalling of depreciation charges for non-current assets based on standard rates of depreciation.

It is still important to maintain a high level of professional scepticism in relation to the results of automated procedures because they can be configured incorrectly or could fail completely if there is a system error. The results should be checked on regular basis to ensure the automation is operating as expected.

Task 2.9

Plant and machinery cost account

	£		£
Balance b/d	40,246		
Cash book	522,730	Balance c/d	562,976
Total	562,976	Total	562,976

Task 2.10

Description	Impact	Amount £
Statement of financial position	Increase non-current assets	1,034,600
Statement of profit or loss	Reduce profit	17,400

When a business buys a non-current asset, the purchase price plus directly attributable costs are capitalised. The amount to be capitalised as a non-current asset in the statement of financial position is £1,034,500 (£1,000,000 + £30,000 + £4,600).

The repairs are revenue expenditure rather than capital expenditure and therefore, the £17,400 should be recorded as an expense in the statement of profit or loss. This will have the effect of reducing profit.

Task 2.11

The correct answers are:

	✓
Assistant requesting the equipment	
Supervisor	
Manager	✓
Company Director	✓

£1,200 is below the limit for the manager and for the director, but over the authorisation limit for the supervisor.

Non-current assets are often some of the most expensive items a business will purchase. It is imperative this expenditure is appropriately authorised prior to the item being purchased.

Authorisation will help ensure assets are not bought unnecessarily and are acquired at the best prices and on the best terms.

Task 2.12

The correct answers are:

	✓
The non-current asset register is always maintained separately and independently from the information in the accounting software.	
Postings for depreciation are only made in the general ledger but not in the non-current asset register.	
Acquisitions and disposals need to be reflected in both the general ledger and non-current asset register.	✓
A control adopted by companies to help detect errors is to periodically reconcile the non-current asset register to the relevant general ledger accounts.	✓

The non-current asset register can be incorporated into the accounting software or it may be held on separate software such as in spreadsheets.

Acquisitions, disposals and depreciation should all be reflected in both the general ledger and on the non-current asset register.

An accountant is likely to reconcile the non-current asset register to the relevant general ledger accounts on a regular basis in order to confirm the accuracy of the accounting records.

Task 2.13

(a) The company made a [loss on disposal] of £ [4,614] on the part exchanged asset.

Disposals account

	£		£
Plant and equipment cost	43,800	Plant and equipment accumulated depreciation	5,586
		Plant and equipment cost	33,600
		Statement of profit or loss	**4,614**
Total	43,800	Total	43,800

(b) £ [37,680]

List price + VAT = £59,400 × 120% = £71,280

Deduct trade in allowance of £33,600 = £37,680 paid by bank transfer.

Task 2.14

(a) £ [24,852]

The depreciation is calculated as:

(£155,016 − £30,756) × 0.2 = £24,852

(b) Debit [Depreciation expense]

Credit [Accumulated depreciation]

Task 2.15

(a) Prepaid expenses

	£		£
Balance b/d	3,000	Rent expense	3,000
Rent expense	4,000	Balance c/d	4,000
Total	7,000	Total	7,000

Rent expense DR = 3/6 × £8,000 = £4,000

(b) The adjustment to record the accrued expense will [increase] current liabilities in the statement of financial position.

This will be a credit to the accrued expense account (accruals), increasing current liabilities. The expense account will be debited decreasing profit for the year.

Task 2.16

The balance for the allowance for doubtful receivables is £ 6,000 .

The calculation is £100,000 × 6% = £6,000.

You have been asked for the year end position only for the allowance for doubtful receivables. The irrecoverable debt which has been written off has already been accounted for and does not require adjusting.

The expense to profit or loss in respect of irrecoverable debts would be Nil, comprising the amount written off of £4,000 (debit) and the decrease in the allowance for doubtful receivables of £4,000 (credit).

Task 2.17

Inventory is measured at the lower of cost and net realisable value, hence being measured at £49.60 per unit in this scenario.

(a) £ 50.20

Working

£49.20 + £1.00

(b) £ 49.60

Working

£51.60 − £2.00

(c) £ 12,400

Working

250 units × £49.60

Task 2.18

The correct answers are:

	✓
Payments made to suppliers not reflected in the payables ledger control account entries.	✓
A supplier missing from the list of suppliers in the subsidiary payables ledger.	
A credit note entered on the wrong side of a suppliers account in the subsidiary ledger.	
An incorrect total posted to payables ledger control account.	✓

Only incorrect entries in the control account or transactions missing from the control account are relevant here. Adjusting the subsidiary ledgers won't need a correction in the control account if the error only exists in the manual subsidiary records that sit outside the general ledger.

Task 2.19

The correct answer is:

	✓
True	
False	✓

Some errors (compensating, or errors of omission for example) exist that don't result in a difference on the trial balance so won't result in a suspense account balance. Accounting procedures still need to be carried out to detect and correct any errors that may still exist.

Task 2.20

The correct answer is:

	✓
True	
False	✓

Timing differences do not need to be adjusted in the cash book.

Task 2.21

The statement of profit or loss provide(s) a summary of the income and expenses incurred by the business over a period of time.

The statement of financial position list(s) all of the assets, liabilities and capital of the business on the period-end date of the accounting period.

Task 2.22

£ 676,000

This is calculated as £520,000/100 × 130 = £676,000.

Chapter 3 – Management Accounting Techniques (MATS)

Task 3.1

(a) The correct answers are:

	✓
Controlling the organisation	✓
Meeting legal requirements	
Planning future operations	✓
Management decision making	✓

Management information is used for planning, controlling and decision making purposes. There is no legal requirement for management information.

(b) The correct answer is:

	✓
Valuing inventory	
Preparing a budget	✓
Selecting the most appropriate investment	
Analysing variances	

Preparing a budget is part of an organisation's planning process. Selecting an investment is decision making activity and analysing variances is a control activity. Valuing inventory is an activity associated with costing.

(c) The correct answers are:

	✓
Direct labour	✓
Direct material	✓
Direct expenses	✓
Production overheads	
Selling and distribution overheads	

A product's prime cost is the total of its direct costs. Prime cost plus production overheads is the total production cost of the product. The total cost of the product is the total production cost plus non-financial overheads (such as selling a distribution overheads).

Task 3.2

(a) £ 75

Lothar's overtime rate per hour = 20 × 1.25 = 25

Overtime premium is the additional cost of overtime hours above the basic rate. For Lothar this is £75 ((£25 – £20) × 15).

(b) The correct answer is:

Direct cost	
Indirect cost	✓

Lothar's overtime would only be treated as a direct cost if it is attributable to a particular customer order or if it is worked regularly (in which case it would be included in the normal hourly wage rate).

(c) The correct answer is:

DR Wages control CR Production	
DR Wages control CR Production overheads	
DR Production CR Wages control	✓
DR Production overheads CR Wages control	

Direct labour costs are production costs, not production overheads. Double entry is to CR the Wages control account with the value of the direct labour cost and to DR Production.

(d) The correct answer is:

Production overhead control account	
Production control account	✓

Direct material costs are recorded in the production control account. Indirect material costs are recorded in the production overhead control account.

(e) The correct answer is:

As a production cost	
As a production overhead	
As a non-production cost	
As a non-production overhead	✓

All businesses will buy some sort of goods for consumption, which are generally classified as indirect materials and included in overheads. In a manufacturing business, such as Natwich Ltd, machine spare parts and lubricants would be production overheads, while office stationery (such as printer consumables) would be a non-production overhead.

(f) The correct answer is:

	✓
DR Production £17,500, CR Production overheads £17,500	✓
DR Production overheads £17,500, CR Production £17,500	
DR Production £17,500, CR Statement of profit or loss £17,500	
DR Production overheads £17,500, CR Statement of profit or loss £17,500	

The production overheads account already has a debit balance from the initial entry. By recording the actual amount of the overhead which is absorbed, the account will be left with a credit balance of £2,500 which will now need to be journaled to the statement of profit or loss.

(g) The correct answer is:

	✓
The production overhead was over-absorbed	✓
The production overhead was under-absorbed	
The production overhead was neither over nor under absorbed	

The actual cost of the overhead was £15,000 and Kilofish Ltd absorbed £17,500 during production. Therefore it over-absorbed the overhead by £2,500.

Task 3.3

(a) The correct answer is:

	✓
Fixed	
Variable	✓
Stepped	

Variable costs change directly in relation to changes in production volume. Fixed costs are unaffected by production volume. Stepped costs are fixed over small ranges of production volume.

(b) The correct answer is:

	✓
Fixed	
Variable	
Stepped	
Semi-variable	✓

Mobile phone bills usually have a fixed and variable element. For example, a fixed cost for an allowance which includes call and data charges up to a particular amount and a variable cost for calls and data once the allowance has been used up. This makes it a semi-variable cost.

(c) The correct answer is:

	✓
Variable	
Stepped	
Fixed	✓
Semi-variable	

The graph shows a fixed cost. Because the cost fixed, as it is spread over more units of output, the cost per unit falls.

Task 3.4

(a) The correct answers are:

	✓
There is no price list	✓
There is no standard product	✓
Each job will have different costs	✓
It is often used by service organisations	

Jobbing businesses (such as builders, plumbers and electricians) have no price list as such and no standard product. The requirements for each customer will different and therefore each individual job will be different with different costs. Service organisations would use service costing.

(b) The correct answer is:

	✓
Batch costing	
Job costing	
Service costing	✓
Process costing	

A composite cost unit is a cost unit where the service combines more than one activity. Organisations in the service industry often use composite cost units to analyse and monitor their costs, particularly when a 'single' cost unit would not be appropriate.

(c) 50 litres

Normal loss is 5%, so for this process, the normal loss is 50 litres (1,000 × 5%)

(d) The correct answer is:

	✓
Abnormal loss	✓
Abnormal gain	

In this process, the normal loss is 50 litres. The actual loss was 66 litres (1,000 – 934). Therefore, the actual loss was greater than the normal loss, which indicates an abnormal loss. An abnormal gain would have resulted if the actual loss was less than 50 (less than the normal loss).

Task 3.5

(a) To calculate the direct labour cost for a cost unit, you multiply the number of labour hours needed to produce one unit by the labour rate per hour.

The direct labour cost per unit is calculated by multiplying the number of labour hours needed to produce one unit by the labour rate per hour.

(b) 73,684 kg

Total materials needed for production = 10,000 × 7 = 70,000 kg

Additional materials needed for wastage = 70,000 × 5/95 = 3,684 kg

Total materials needed = 73,684 kg

(c) A master budget is an example of a fixed budget

An example of a fixed budget is the master budget prepared before the beginning of the budget period.

(d) Direct material costs for 500 units are £ 500 and for 750 units are £ 750

Factory rates for 500 units are £ 75,000 and for 750 units are £ 75,000

Direct material costs will change with production levels (£1 per unit of output). Factory rates are fixed and will not be affected by changes in production levels.

(e) The correct answer is:

	✓
True	✓
False	

A rolling budget is compiled by adding the next accounting period when the current accounting period is over. By doing this, a set amount of time is always included within the budget.

Task 3.6

(a)

	Budgeted (£)	Actual (£)	Variance (£)	Adverse/ Favourable
Materials	220,375	202,578	17,797	Favourable

The actual cost of the materials is less than budget, therefore it is a favourable variance.

(b) The correct answers are:

	✓
Careless purchasing	✓
Increase in idle time	
Lack of staff training in production teams	
Theft	✓
Stricter quality control	✓

Examples of causes of adverse materials variances include:

- Price increase
- Careless purchasing
- Defective material
- Excessive waste or theft
- Stricter quality control
- Errors in allocating material to jobs

Increase in idle time and lack of staff training are possible causes of adverse labour variances.

(c) The total variable overhead variance is the difference between the [actual cost of variable overhead] for the period and the [budgeted cost of variable overhead] for the [actual production in the period].

The total variable overhead variance is the difference between the actual cost of variable overhead for the period and the budgeted cost of variable overhead for the actual production in the period.

(d) The sales price variance is the difference between the [actual revenue received] and the [budgeted revenue received] for the [actual level of sales].

The sales price variance is the difference between the actual revenue received and the budgeted revenue received for the actual level of sales.

Task 3.7

(a) £ 215,560

In March, the company will not receive any cash from March sales. It will receive 80% of the sales from one month ago (February) and 20% of the sales from two months ago (January).

£225,575 × 80% = £180,460

£175,500 × 20% = £35,100

£180,460 + £35,100 = £215,560

(b) The correct answers are:

	✓
Costs	✓
Profits	✓
Investments	

A manager of a profit centre is responsible for the centre's costs and profit. A manager of a cost centre is just responsible for costs and the manager of an investment centre is responsible for costs, profits and investments.

(c) The ⎡principal budget factor⎤ limits an organisation's performance for a given period and is often the starting point in budget preparation.

The master budget consists of a budgeted statement of profit or loss, a budgeted statement of financial position and a cash budget.

(d) It is important for the motivation of responsibility centre managers that they are only accountable for ⎡controllable costs⎤.

Managers of responsibility centres should only be held accountable for costs over which they have some influence. From a motivation point of view, this is important because it can be very demoralising for managers who feel that their performance is being judged on the basis of something over which they have no influence. It is also important from a control point of view in that control reports should ensure that information on costs is reported to the manager who is able to take action to control them.

(e) The correct answer is:

	✓
True	
False	✓

Although the purchase of the asset impacts the statement of financial position. A depreciation charge will need to be budgeted for which will impact the statement of profit or loss.

(f) The correct answer is:

	✓
True	
False	✓

Capital income is the proceeds from the sale of non-trading assets (ie proceeds from the sale of non-current assets, including investments). The profits (or losses) from the sale are included in the statement of profit or loss for the accounting period in which the sale takes place.

Revenue income is derived from the following sources:

- The sale of trading assets
- Interest and dividends received from investments held by the business

Task 3.8

(a) The correct answers are:

	Cash item ✓	Non-cash item ✓
Accruals concept		✓
Owner's capital received	✓	
Provisions for future expenses		✓
Sale of office equipment	✓	

Accruals and provisions are accounting principles that allocate costs or revenues between different accounting periods. They do not affect cash. Capital received from owners and from sale of assets both will involve money being paid into the business' bank account.

(b) The correct answer is:

	✓
Shares purchased from the stock exchange	
Cash held in fixed term investments	
Trade receivables	✓
Cash at bank	

Assets are more liquid as they become easier and quicker to convert into cash. Cash is the most liquid asset followed by shares (which can quickly be sold on the stock exchange). Cash in fixed term investments can only be converted into cash once the fixed term of the investment has expired. Trade receivables are the least liquid because the business must wait until the customer pays what they owe, which in some cases may be never.

(c) [130] days

The inventory holding period is calculated as (inventory/cost of sales) × 365

(3,766 / 10,575) × 365 = 130

(d) [57] days

The working capital cycle is calculated as:

Trade receivables days + inventory holding period − trade payables days

37 + 60 − 40 = 57

(e) The correct answer is:

	✓
Chase late-paying customers	✓
Pay suppliers earlier	
Sell non-current assets	
Increase inventory levels	

To reduce the working capital cycle, the business should look for ways to: reduce the time that it takes to collect what it is owed, reduce the time inventory is held for before being sold, or to pay suppliers later.

Paying suppliers earlier would increase rather than reduce the working capital cycle. Selling non-current assets would not impact the working capital cycle because it will not affect the trade receivables payment period, inventory holding period, or trade payables payment period. Increasing inventory levels will not in itself reduce the working capital cycle and may even increase it unless there is a corresponding or greater increase in cost of sales.

Chapter 4 – Business Awareness (BUAW)

Task 4.1

(a) The correct answers are:

Stakeholder	Internal ✓	Connected ✓	External ✓
Shareholders		✓	
Suppliers		✓	
Directors	✓		
Competitors			✓

Stakeholders can be classified as:

Internal:

- Corporate management (eg directors)
- Employees

Connected:

- Shareholders
- Debt holders (eg bank)
- Intermediate (business) and final (consumer) customers
- Suppliers

External:

- Immediate community/ Society at large
- Competitors
- Special interest groups
- Government

(b) The correct answers are:

Statement	True ✓	False ✓
Mendelow's matrix helps an organisation to assess each stakeholder's likely reaction to a business decision	✓	
Mendelow's matrix helps an organisation to evaluate actions that may ease the acceptance of a business decision	✓	

Mendelow's matrix is a useful tool in helping organisations to:

- Identify stakeholders who are likely to be affected by a particular decision.
- Assess each stakeholder's likely reaction to the decision eg support/neutral/object.
- Evaluate the policies or actions that may ease the acceptance of the strategy.

(c) The correct answer is:

	✓
Agatha, who has low interest and low power in the organisation	
Bjorn, who has high interest and low power in the organisation	
Cynthia, who has high power and low interest in the organisation	✓
Drake, who has high power and high interest in the organisation	

According to Mendelow's matrix:

- Agatha should be treated with 'minimal effort'
- Bjorn should be 'kept informed'
- Cynthia should be 'kept satisfied'
- Drake should be treated as a 'key player'

	Level of interest	
Power	**Low**	**High**
Low	A eg Casual labour Action: **Minimal effort**	B eg Core employees Action: **Keep informed**
High	C eg Institutional shareholder Action: **Keep satisfied**	D eg Main suppliers Action: **Key players**

Task 4.2

(a) The correct answers are:

Statement	True ✓	False ✓
Sustainability is only a concern of the special interest groups of an organisation's stakeholders		✓
Sustainability requires organisations to carefully consider how they manage resources	✓	
Sustainability requires a company to take a holistic view	✓	
Sustainability requires companies to adopt a short-term view of profits		✓

Most stakeholders will have an interest in sustainability, not just special interest groups. Resource management and taking an holistic view are key sustainability issues for organisations. Sustainability requires companies to adopt a long-term (not short-term) view of profits

(b) The correct answers are:

Business activity	Social justice ✓	Environmental quality ✓	Economic prosperity ✓
Offsetting carbon emissions		✓	
Being a good corporate citizen	✓		
Paying a fair share of tax			✓

Social justice – being a good corporate citizen. This can be evidenced by good employment practices.

Environmental quality – striving to be environmentally neutral, eg planting trees to offset wood used in the production process.

Economic prosperity – creating and sharing the economic wealth generated, eg shunning aggressive tax avoidance schemes, instead choosing to pay your 'fair share' of tax on your corporate profits.

Task 4.3

(a) The correct answers are:

	True ✓	False ✓
'I know I act ethically as I have never broken the law and always comply with regulations.'		✓
'The AAT Code of Professional Ethics is legally binding if you are a member of the AAT.'		✓

Complying with laws and regulations does not ensure your actions are ethical. They are the minimum standard of behaviour expected by society. Acting ethically means to go beyond this. There is no legal requirement to follow the AAT Code of Professional Ethics.

(b) The correct answer is:

	✓
Familiarity	✓
Self-interest	
Advocacy	

The family connection creates a familiarity threat.

(c) The correct answer is:

	✓
Integrity	
Objectivity	✓
Confidentiality	

There would be a conflict of interest if Rajesh carries out this work which would affect his objectivity.

(d) The correct answer is:

	✓
Resign from RMS Accountancy	
Inform RMS Accountancy of his link with Carmichael Ltd	✓
Inform the AAT of his link with Carmichael Ltd	

Resigning is not necessary when notifying his employer could resolve the situation (the client could be moved to someone else). The AAT do not need to be notified.

(e) The correct answer is:

	✓
Leaders of the firm have issued clear policies on the ethical behaviour expected at RMS Accountancy.	
Leaders of the firm demonstrate the importance of compliance with the fundamental principles.	✓
Leaders of the firm require that any potential threat to the fundamental principles is communicated to them in order for the most appropriate action to be taken.	

The tone-at-the-top means that an organisation's leadership embody and demonstrate the ethical standards that they expect employees to follow.

(f) The correct answers are:

Statement	True ✓	False ✓
'The AAT Code of Professional Ethics does not apply to me yet as I am only a student accounting technician.'		✓
'Ethical codes provide advice as to how to comply with the law.'	✓	

The AAT Code of Ethics applies to students and full members alike. Because compliance with the law is a minimum standard of behaviour expected of accountants, following an ethical code should mean that the accountant is also complying with the law.

(g) If you have an ethical concern at work, usually the most appropriate first course of action would be to raise this with an employee helpline.

Raising the matter with a trusted colleague may breach confidentiality. The most appropriate place to go is a helpline that is provided by your employer. Otherwise, the AAT could also be contacted as a last resort providing confidentiality is not at risk.

(h) The correct answers are:

	✓
Providing working papers to a new firm who is taking on a former client	✓
As a result of an enquiry by AAT	✓
To a financial institution who has requested the information directly from your firm of accountants	
To protect a member's professional interest in a court of law	✓

Before supplying information to a financial institution, the permission of the person who is the subject of the information should be sought.

Task 4.4

(a) The correct answer is:

	✓
Layering	
Placement	✓
Integration	

The money laundering process usually comprises of three distinct phases:

(1) Placement – the disposal of the proceeds of crime into an apparently legitimate business property or activity.

(2) Layering – the transfer of money from place to place, in order to conceal its criminal origins.

(3) Integration – the culmination of placement and layering, giving the money the appearance of being from a legitimate source.

(b) The correct answer is:

	✓
No, she was unaware of being involved in money laundering and withdrew from the engagement as soon as she suspected wrong doing.	
No, the money laundering scheme was very small scale and would therefore be below the threshold for criminal conviction.	
Yes, if she has been part of the scheme, even unknowingly, she could still be guilty of money laundering.	✓

There is no threshold for criminal conviction and ignorance of what is going on is no excuse. This is why accountants have to be very wary of situations which may indicate money laundering is occurring.

(c) The correct answers are:

Statement	True ✓	False ✓
Rita has tipped off the client.		✓
If Rita does fail to disclose her suspicions of money laundering she may face additional charges.	✓	

Telling someone you will have no further dealings with them is not an example of tipping off. To tip off, Rita would have had to tell the person that she is reporting them to the authorities. Failure to disclose suspicions is a money laundering offence.

(d) The correct answers are:

Statement	True ✓	False ✓
Alfred is required to report his suspicions to the AAT		✓
Failure to disclose money laundering suspicions can result in imprisonment	✓	
Alfred must ensure that he makes François aware that the relevant disclosures have been made.		✓

Alfred should report his suspicions to his firm's nominated officer or money laundering reporting officer – not the AAT. The penalty for failing to disclose suspicions of money laundering is up to 5 years in prison and/or a fine. Alfred must not tell François about his disclosures, otherwise he will be committing the tipping off offence.

Task 4.5

(a) **Blockchain** is one form of distributed ledger technology.

Blockchain is one form of distributed ledger technology. It is a way of recording transactions in 'blocks' which are linked to one another and secured against being altered using cryptography, based on complex calculations. Any party who has owned the asset can view the previous transaction data, but this information is not necessarily otherwise shared or publicly available.

(b) The correct answer is:

	✓
Value	
Veracity	
Variety	✓
Volume	
Velocity	

Big data has five characteristics:

Volume – the quantity of data that is available.

Velocity – the speed at which big data can be accessed by an organisation.

Variety – the different forms that big data can take.

Veracity – the trustworthiness or accuracy of big data.

Value – the ability of big data to add value to an organisation.

(c) The correct answer is:

	✓
Blockchain	
Robotic process automation	
Artificial intelligence	✓
Cloud accounting	

Artificial intelligence can help speed up data analytics by finding patterns in data.

(d) When a service provider uses public cloud resources to create their private cloud, the result is called a virtual private cloud.

When a service provider uses public cloud resources to create their private cloud, the result is called a virtual private cloud.

(e) The correct answers are:

	✓
Fully managed	✓
On-demand and self-service	✓
Sold on demand	✓
Elastic	✓

These are all characteristics of cloud computing.

(f) Rita is a data processor.

Greenhub Ltd is a data controller.

Keisha is a data subject

Tiltwood plc is not a data subject

Organisations that process personal data (such as Greenhub Ltd) are known as Data controllers. Data processors (Rita) are responsible for processing personal data on behalf of a controller. Data subjects are identified or identifiable individuals (such as Keisha), but not companies (such as Tiltwood plc) to whom personal data relates.

(g) The correct answers are:

Description	Correct ✓	Incorrect ✓
The principle of purpose limitation means that organisations are limited to using data in accordance with their vision, mission and corporate objectives.		✓
The principle of storage limitation means that organisations can only store that data in government approved systems.		✓
The principle of data minimisation means that data held by organisations must be adequate, relevant and not excessive.	✓	
The principle of lawfulness, fairness, and transparency means that there must be valid grounds for holding the data.	✓	

The principle of purpose limitation means that the purpose for recording the data must be recorded and made clear to the data subject from the start.

The principle of storage limitation means that data should not be kept for longer than is necessary for the purpose for which it was processed.

The principle of data minimisation means that data held must be adequate (sufficient to fulfil the purpose), relevant (linked rationally to the purpose) and not excessive.

The principle of lawfulness, fairness, and transparency means that there must be valid grounds for holding the data.

(h) The correct answers are:

Description	Distributed denial of service attack (DDoS) ✓	Ransomware ✓
Bots are instructed to overwhelm the organisation's website with a wave of internet traffic so that the system is unable to handle it and may crash	✓	
The cyber-attacker gains access to the user's system to lock their files and prevent access to them.		✓

In a denial of service attack, the cyber-attacker attempts to disrupt an organisation's online activities by preventing people from accessing the organisation's website. Bots are instructed to overwhelm the organisation's website with a wave of internet traffic so that the system is unable to handle it and may crash.

In ransomware (file hijacker) attacks, the cyber-attacker gains access to the user's system to hijack their files and hold them to ransom.

(i) Patch management is a form of cyber security which involves updating software with uploads to fix security issues.

The most common types of cyber security include:

Access controls – passwords or locked doors to prevent access to systems

Boundary firewalls – software to regulate/monitor access to internal systems by outside sources

Malware protection – software to prevent hacking tools being uploaded to systems

Patch management – uploads to fix security issues with existing software

Task 4.6

(a) The correct answers are:

Characteristic	Strategic level ✓	Operational level ✓
Unstructured	✓	
Mainly internally sourced		✓
Short-term focus		✓

Strategic level information will be largely:

- Unstructured – no consistent format
- Externally sourced
- Focused on the long-term strategy of the business

Operational level information will be largely:

- Structured, eg sales and inventory reports
- Internally sourced
- Focused on the daily, weekly or monthly operational processes

(b) The correct answer is:

	✓
Understandable	
Easy to use	
Relevant	✓
Accurate	

Relevant information reflects the needs of the user. For example, it provides just the information that the person needs to make a decision.

Understandable information is provided in a format that the user can understand. For example, it avoids technical jargon.

Easy-to-use information is presented in a medium appropriate to the user. For example in a report, email or spreadsheet.

Accurate information is technically correct and all calculations work mathematically. Information should be as accurate as the user needs it to be (ie some loss of accuracy might be tolerated if the information is provided quickly).

(c) The correct answer is:

	✓
Technically correct	
Achieving its purpose	
Clearly understandable	✓
Professionally presented	

Clearly understandable means that the communication is tailored to the writer's purpose in communicating (so that a clear message is sent) and to the information needs, language and capabilities of its audience (so that the message can be received).

Technically correct means to ensure that content is accurate, appropriately detailed (for different levels of requirement) and checked for factual/data and typographical errors.

Achieving its purpose means to obtain feedback to check that the communication has been effective. Has it 'done its job'? Has it got the response it aimed for? If not: adjust and try again!

Professionally presented means to ensure that documents are neat, legible, concise, helpfully structured and smartly presented: showing competence and awareness of business needs.

(d) The correct answer is:

	✓
True	
False	✓

Data visualisation is a computer-based tool used to present data through dashboards and mapping charts rather than in printed reports.

(e) The correct answers are:

	✓
Information must be generated as close to the time it is needed for decision making.	
Patterns and anomalies in the data are easy to spot	✓
Information can be drilled into	✓
Data visualisation supports efficient decision making	✓

Real-time processing means the information is always kept up-to-date so does not have to be generated close to the time it is needed.

(f) The correct answers are:

Description	Bar chart ✓	Line graph ✓
Useful for showing or comparing magnitudes or sizes of items	✓	
Useful for showing the relationship between two variables		✓

Bar charts are useful for showing or comparing magnitudes or sizes of items: for example, unit sales of each product each month over the financial year.

Line graphs are useful for showing the relationship between two variables (represented by the horizontal and vertical axes of the graph), by plotting points and joining them up with straight or curved lines. These are particularly useful for demonstrating trends, such as the variation in unit sales each month.

(g) Matrix diagrams show the relationship between items.

Matrix diagrams show the relationship between items. These allow you to quickly assess the value of certain items relative to each other.

Pie charts are useful for showing the relative sizes of component elements of a total value or amount, represented by the 360 degrees of the circle or 'pie'.

Tables are a good way of organising information. The use of columns and rows allows the data to be classified under appropriate headings, clearly organised and labelled, totalled up in various ways (across rows or down columns) and so on.

AAT Practice Assessment

EPA Knowledge Assessment

You are advised to attempt practice assessments online from the AAT website. This will ensure you are prepared for how the assessment will be presented on the AAT's system when you attempt the real assessment. Please access the assessment using the address below:

https://www.aat.org.uk/training/study-support/search

The AAT may call the assessments on their website, under study support resources, either a 'practice assessment' or 'sample assessment'.

BPP Practice Assessment 1

EPA Knowledge Assessment

Time allowed: 2 hours 30 mins (90 minutes for the assessment and a further 60 minutes for reflection and planning as needed)

EPA Knowledge Assessment
BPP Practice Assessment 1

Assessment information

You have **2 hours and 30 minutes** to complete this practice assessment.

- This assessment contains **3 tasks** and you should attempt to complete every task.
- Each task is independent. You will not need to refer to your answers to previous tasks.
- The total number of marks for this assessment is **40**.
- Read every task carefully to make sure you understand what is required.
- Where the date is relevant, it is given in the task data.
- Both minus signs and brackets can be used to indicate negative numbers unless task instructions state otherwise.
- You must use a full stop to indicate a decimal point. For example, write 100.57 not 100,57 or 10057.
- You may use a comma to indicate a number in the thousands, but you don't have to. For example, 10000 and 10,000 are both acceptable.

Task 1 (20 marks)

You are the Accounts Assistant for Company A, which manufacturers smartphones.

You are preparing transactions, reconciling control accounts and amending any errors in the financial records ready to prepare the financial statements for the year ended 31 March 20X4.

Company A is VAT registered and your supervisor has asked you some questions on VAT that they would like you to answer as part of the year end process.

You are also training a new employee who has limited experience of preparing financial records. Going forward they will be helping out with management accounting tasks.

Today's date is 24 April 20X4.

Company A made sales of £2,400 at a promotional event. During the event, the buyers all paid in cash for the smart phones which were all sold at a discounted price for the purposes of the promotion.

Required

(a) Which book of prime entry should the sales be recorded in?

	✓
Discounts allowed daybook	
Sales daybook	
Cash book	
Discounts received daybook	

(1 mark)

Company A does not use all of the parking spaces available in the car park it owns, so it rents out the surplus spaces to a nearby business (Company P) for £300 per quarter.

You have noticed that the invoice to company P for the quarter ended 31 March 20X4 was not raised until 2 April 20X4 but the rental income for the car parking spaces was recorded on 31 March 20X4 using a journal.

Required

(b) The journal entered in respect of the rental of the car parking spaces was to record which of the following?

	✓
Prepaid income	
Accrued income	
Prepaid expense	
Accrued expense	

(1 mark)

As part of your year-end review, you are assessing depreciation rates to ensure they are reasonable based on the useful lives of the assets.

Required

(c) Which accounting principle are you complying with by carrying out this review?

[▼]

Picklist

- Accruals
- Going concern
- Money measurement
- Prudence

(1 mark)

Company A has a customer who has an unpaid invoice which is still outstanding.

Required

(d) Which of the following is one of the valid conditions needed to reclaim VAT that has been paid as bad debt relief?

	✓
The customer must have repaid the input tax to HMRC	
Output tax has been paid and accounted for	
10 months must have elapsed since the payment was due	
The debt has not yet been written off in the VAT account of Company A	

(1 mark)

Extracts from the accounting records of Company A are as follows. You are trying to calculate the depreciation charge for the year ended 31 March 20X4.

Account	Debit £	Credit £
Land and buildings – cost	2,400,000	
Office equipment – cost	11,200	
Office equipment – accumulated depreciation at 1 April 20X3		2,600

On 1 April 20X3, Company A purchased the land and buildings at a total cost of £2,400,000. The land had a cost of £1,500,000 and the buildings cost £900,000.

The cost of office equipment at 31 March 20X3 was £10,400. Additions to office equipment are a photocopier and scanner with a total cost of £800 purchased on 15 January 20X4.

The depreciation policy of Company A is as follows:

- land is not depreciated
- buildings are depreciated on a straight-line basis over an expected useful life of 30 years
- office equipment is depreciated on a diminishing balance basis at 25%

Assets are depreciated on an annual basis with a full year's depreciation charged in the year of acquisition.

Required

(e) (i) Calculate the depreciation for the year ended 31 March 20X4 relating to the land and buildings.

Land and buildings depreciation: £ [ ] (1 mark)

(ii) Calculate the depreciation for the year ended 31 March 20X4 relating to the office equipment.

Office equipment depreciation: £ [ ] (1 mark)

Your new employee is looking at invoices related to an item of property, plant and equipment (a machine used in the manufacture of smartphones) delivered earlier in the year.

Required

(iii) In addition to the cost of the machine, which of the following costs should be capitalised under IAS 16 Property, Plant and Equipment?

	✓
Costs incurred in researching the best machine for the intended purpose	
Machine delivery costs	
VAT charged at 20% of the cost of the machine.	
Cost of contract for maintenance of the machinery for one year	

(1 mark)

Your supervisor is considering the VAT implications of proposed purchases in April 20X4 and has asked you about certain VAT rules.

Company A will pay £3,250 for a new piece of standard rated equipment.

Required

(f) (i) Calculate the VAT that will be incurred. Show your answer to two decimal places.

£ [ ] (1 mark)

A purchase invoice for taxable supplies has been received and recorded in the general ledger.

Required

(ii) Which ONE of the following states the effect of the invoice received on VAT?

	✓
Input tax will increase	
Input tax will decrease	
Output tax will increase	
Output tax will decrease	

(1 mark)

The VAT figures for Company A for the VAT period ended 31 March 20X4 have been extracted below. All previous VAT liabilities have been settled.

	£
Sales invoices	9,520.50
Purchase invoices	10,410.40
Purchase credit notes	3,120.80

Required

(g) (i) Calculate the amount of the VAT due.

VAT: £ ☐ (1 mark)

(ii) Identify whether the amount due is due TO or due FROM HMRC.

The VAT is ☐▼ HMRC.

Picklist
- Due to be paid to
- Due to be refunded by

(1 mark)

You have been asked to check the June 20X4 materials budget.

For June 20X3, purchases of mobile phone screens was £375,869. The cost of these screens is forecast to fall by 5% for the year to June 20X4.

Required

(h) Calculate the materials budget for mobile phone screens for June 20X4. Show your answer to two decimal places.

£ ☐ (1 mark)

Each mobile phone has a case which is made from plastic that is melted down and poured into moulds. Each mobile phone case requires 180 grams of plastic and there is a normal loss of 10% in the process.

Required

(i) Calculate how many grams of plastic is needed for each mobile phone case.

☐ grams (1 mark)

(j) Which type of cost increases with every additional unit of production?

☐▼

Picklist
- Fixed
- Stepped
- Variable

(1 mark)

When reviewing the accounting records for March 20X4 you find that a page in the purchases daybook totalling £1,872 was omitted from the general ledger. The balance on the payables ledger control account at 31 March 20X4 was £5,894.

Required

(k) Complete the following statement.

The entry to amend the error will [▼] the balance on the payables ledger control account. The payables ledger control account is a [▼] balance in the general ledger.

Picklist
- Credit
- Debit
- Decrease
- Increase

(2 marks)

You are reviewing the March 20X4 payroll for Company A to ensure any liabilities to HRMC have been calculated properly. Employee X is paid their monthly salary on 28th of each month and their employment contract specifies an annual salary of £42,000.

The payroll has generated the following report for employee X for the month of March 20X4:

	£
Income tax	490
Employee's NIC	196
Employer's NIC	378
Employee's pension contributions	105
Employer's pension contributions	140

Required

(l) Complete the following sentences:

The net pay for employee X for March 20X4 is £ [____]

Company A must pay £ [____] to HMRC in respect of employee X for the month of March 20X4

(2 marks)

When looking at invoices leading up to March 20X4, you notice Company A received an invoice for telephone expenses on 1 March 20X4. The bill showed telephone expenses of £1,800 covering the period from 1 March 20X4 to 31 May 20X4.

Required

(m) Select the correct journal entry in respect of the telephone expenses.

	✓
DR Telephone expense £600, CR Prepayments £600	
DR Prepayments £1,200, CR Telephone expense £1,200	
DR Telephone expense £1,200 CR Accruals £1,200	
DR Accruals £600, CR Telephone expense £600	

(1 mark)

Your trainee asks you how prepaid income (deferred income) is recognised in the financial statements.

Required

(n) Complete the following statement.

Prepaid income should be recognised as [▼] in the statement of financial position.

Picklist
- A current asset
- A current liability
- A non-current asset
- Equity

(1 mark)

Task 2 (10 marks)

Company A has recently appointed a new Finance Director. Under the direction of the new Finance Director, the company is carrying out a review of its accounting systems and processes.

As the accounts assistant, you have been asked to research the options and help provide useful information to help decide on the best approach going forward. This includes any technology the business can make use of while making sure any relevant legislation is complied with, such as protecting personal data.

You are also reviewing the final accounts, including the VAT position and amounts due to HMRC, in addition to addressing any late queries as they arise.

Required

(a) Which of the following is NOT a feature of cloud accounting software?

	✓
Simultaneous access by multiple users	
Supports flexible working practices	
Operates separately from other business systems	
Automatic software updates	

(1 mark)

Company A is looking to offer some employees the opportunity to work at home rather than at the office.

Required

(b) Which of the following would you recommend Company A invests in as a secure place for home-working employees to store their work?

	✓
Mini servers for each employee	
Extra-large hard drives for PCs	
Cloud-based storage	
Large capacity memory sticks	

(1 mark)

(c) Complete the sentence below.

Data in [▼] can be drilled into.

Picklist
- Mapping charts
- Matrices
- Tables

(1 mark)

(d) Identify whether the following statement is true or false.

Data protection legislation does NOT protect data about companies.

	✓
True	
False	

(1 mark)

(e) Which of the following is a cyber security threat?

	✓
Firewall	
Patch management	
Webcam manager	
Access control	

(1 mark)

(f) Which TWO of the following accounts can be either a debit or a credit balance in a trial balance?

	✓
Irrecoverable debts expense account	
Rent receivable account	
Bank general ledger account	
Ordinary share capital account	

(2 marks)

Your company (Company A) offers a 10% discount to customers who pay within 7 days' time.

A customer of Company A purchased a standard rated item which has a net value of £2,300 **before** discount and pays in 5 days.

Required

(g) (i) **Calculate the discounted net value.**

Discounted net value: £ ☐ (1 mark)

(ii) **Calculate the VAT on this standard rated item.**

VAT amount: £ ☐ (1 mark)

Company A has a balance on its receivables ledger control account of £90,000 which includes £2,000 due from a customer that has recently gone into liquidation and is considered irrecoverable. At the end of the previous period, the allowance for doubtful receivables was £1,100. For the current period end, the allowance for doubtful receivables will be 2% of the outstanding trade receivables.

Required

(h) What is the allowance for doubtful receivables adjustment needed to reflect the required position at the current period end?

	✓
£700 increase	
£660 increase	
£700 decrease	
£660 decrease	

(1 mark)

Task 3 (10 marks)

A key responsibility you have been given in your role as Accounts Assistant is reconciling the control accounts to supporting records.

You do this monthly and are responsible for detecting errors and making adjustments where needed.

You have asked your colleague to assist you with the month end bank reconciliation. They have found some differences when comparing the cash book and the bank statements but can't work out which entries, if any, are required to the cash book.

Required

(a) **Identify TWO items that will require an entry in the cash book.**

	✓
A bank error meant a direct debit that was recorded in the cash book was paid twice by the bank, but one payment was refunded by the bank the next day.	
A cheque included in the cash book on the last day of the month did not show on the bank statement until the first week of the following month.	
Interest received showing on the bank statement is not included in the cash book.	
A BACS receipt from a customer is showing on the bank statement but your colleague couldn't find an entry for this in the cash book.	

(2 marks)

You are looking at the bank statement and at the end of the month it shows a credit balance of £2,108.

Required

(b) **Identify whether the following statement is true or false.**

Statement	True ✓	False ✓
If the bank account in the general ledger and the bank statement are in agreement the company financial statements should show a debit balance of £2,108 on the bank account.		

(1 mark)

(c) **Identify whether the following statement is true or false.**

Statement	True ✓	False ✓
Contra entries are adjusted in the receivables ledger control account and payables ledger control account but do not affect the subsidiary receivables and payables ledgers.		

(1 mark)

The payables ledger control account is showing a different balance to the total of the list of individual balances in the payables ledger. You have discovered the difference is due to purchases credit notes received from supplier P Ltd totalling £524 being entered as a credit entry in the payables ledger control account.

Required

(d) **Complete the following statement.**

When you correct this, you should debit the [▼] by £ [   ].

Picklist
- Account of P Ltd
- Payables ledger control account

(2 marks)

A rent payment of £1,200 was posted as a credit to the rent account and a debit to the bank.

Required

(e) Complete the statement below.

When correcting the error made relating to the rent payment, the correcting entry

[▼] result in an entry to the suspense account.

Picklist
- Will
- Will not

(1 mark)

You are reviewing the receivables ledger control account and receivables subsidiary ledger and have picked up some errors in the entries made. The balance on the receivables ledger control account is £18,225.

A credit note issued for £2,122 was only recorded in in Q Ltd's receivable account but was omitted from the general ledger entries.

An invoice for £600 including VAT has been posted to the wrong side of R Ltd's account in the receivables ledger.

You also noticed that the total column in the sales daybook has been undercast by £2,000.

Required

(f) Calculate the correct balance carried down on the receivables ledger control account.

Corrected balance on receivables ledger control account: £ [ ]. *(1 mark)*

Whilst reviewing the bank account, you notice several transactions which look unusual and concern you.

Required

(g) Who should you report this matter to?

[▼]

Picklist
- The Bank
- The Company Treasurer
- The Finance Director
- The Money Laundering Reporting Officer

(1 mark)

(h) If the party in the previous question agrees with your suspicions, who should they file a Suspicious Activity Report with?

	✓
The police	
The National Audit Office	
The National Crime Agency	
The AAT	

(1 mark)

BPP Practice Assessment 1

EPA Knowledge Assessment

Answers

Task 1

(a) The correct answer is:

	✓
Discounts allowed daybook	
Sales daybook	
Cash book	✓
Discounts received daybook	

These were cash sales so they should be recorded in the cash book.

(b) The correct answer is:

	✓
Prepaid income	
Accrued income	✓
Prepaid expense	
Accrued expense	

This is accrued income which is income that has been earned but that has not yet been invoiced or received.

(c) Accruals

Depreciation is a way of spreading the cost of a tangible non-current asset over its useful life. It utilises the accruals principle that the expense should be matched against the benefits generated from using the asset.

(d) The correct answer is:

	✓
The customer must have repaid the input tax to HMRC	
Output tax has been paid and accounted for	✓
10 months must have elapsed since the payment was due	
The debt has not yet been written off in the VAT account of Company A	

Output tax being paid and accounted for is one of the valid conditions when reclaiming VAT that has been paid as bad debt relief. 6 months (not 10) must also have elapsed since payment was due and the debt must have also been written off in the VAT account of the company.

The customer does not need to have already repaid the input VAT in order to reclaim the output tax as bad debt relief.

(e) (i) Land and buildings depreciation: £ 30,000

The land is not depreciated and the buildings are depreciated over 30 years.

Asset	Cost £	Calculation of depreciation	Depreciation charge £
Land	1,500,000	No depreciation	0
Buildings	900,000	= 900k / 30 years	30,000
Total			30,000

(ii) Office equipment depreciation: £ 2,150

The diminishing balance method (25%) is used for depreciation with a full year's depreciation charged in the year of acquisition.

Asset	Amount £	Calculation of depreciation	Depreciation charge £
Carrying amount of Office equipment at 1 April 20X3 (10,400 – 2,600)	7,800	= 7,800 × 25%	1,950
Additions cost	800	= (800 × 25%)	200
Total			2,150

(iii) The correct answer is:

	✓
Costs incurred in researching the best machine for the intended purpose	
Machine delivery costs	✓
VAT charged at 20% of the cost of the machine.	
Cost of contract for maintenance of the machinery for one year	

Costs of researching are not costs that relate directly to the purchase of this specific asset and therefore may not be capitalised.

Delivery can be capitalised as it is necessary to bring the asset to the location and condition necessary for it to be capable of operating in the manner intended by management (IAS 16).

As the business is VAT registered, then the VAT can be reclaimed from the tax authorities. Therefore, the VAT is not capitalised as part of the asset.

The cost of the maintenance contract (£800) should be shown as an expense in the statement of profit or loss as it cannot be capitalised under IAS 16.

(f) (i) £ 541.67

£3,250 × 1/6 = £541.67

(ii) The correct answer is:

	✓
Input tax will increase	✓
Input tax will decrease	
Output tax will increase	
Output tax will decrease	

The VAT on a purchase invoice is input tax so this will increase the overall input tax for the VAT period.

(g) (i) VAT: £ 2230.90

The calculation is shown below

	£
Sales invoices (output tax)	9,520.50
Purchase invoices (input tax)	(10,410.40)
Purchase credit notes (reduction in input tax)	3,120.80
VAT due	2,230.90

(ii) The VAT is due to be paid to HMRC.

The output tax exceeds the input tax (after adjusting for credit notes).

(h) £ 357,075.55

June 20X3 cost was £375,869. This needs to be reduced by 5%.

375,869 × (1 − 0.05) = 357,075.55

(i) 200 grams

180 / 0.9 = 200

(j) Variable

Variable costs increase as production levels increase. Fixed costs fall with every additional unit of production because the same cost is spread over more units. Stepped costs are fixed over small levels of production, but then increase as production volumes reach certain levels.

(k) The entry to amend the error will increase the balance on the payables ledger control account. The payables ledger control account is a credit balance in the general ledger.

The total of the unrecorded invoices will increase the liability to suppliers by £1,872, so the payables ledger control account will need to be credited, increasing the overall credit balance on the payables ledger control to £7,766.

(l) The net pay for employee X for March 20X4 is £ 2,709

Company A must pay £ 1,064 to HMRC in respect of employee X for the month of March 20X4

The net pay is calculated as:

	£
Gross monthly salary (£42,000 / 12)	3,500
Income tax	(490)
Employee's NIC	(196)
Employee's pension contributions	(105)
Net pay	**2,709**

The amount payable to HMRC:

	£
Income tax	490
Employee's NIC	196
Employer's NIC	378
Payable to HMRC	**1,064**

(m) The correct answer is:

	✓
DR Telephone expense £600, CR Prepayments £600	
DR Prepayments £1,200, CR Telephone expense £1,200	✓
DR Telephone expense £1,200 CR Accruals £1,200	
DR Accruals £600, CR Telephone expense £600	

Two months or 2/3 £1,800 = £1,200 has been prepaid. A prepayment is a reduction, or credit to the expense and a prepayment asset (debit) is created.

(n) Prepaid income should be recognised as a current liability in the statement of financial position.

Prepaid income is income that has been received but relates to the following accounting period, ie income received in advance. To temporarily remove the income, the income account in the statement of profit or loss is debited. The balancing entry is a credit of the amount received in advance to a prepaid income (or deferred income) liability account.

Task 2

(a) The correct answer is:

	✓
Simultaneous access by multiple users	
Supports flexible working practices	
Operates separately from other business systems	✓
Automatic software updates	

Cloud accounting improves the integration of software as, for example, customer relationship management software can be linked to accounting software. Simultaneous access by multiple users and from multiple locations (which supports flexible working) are features of cloud accounting software. Cloud-based software can also be updated automatically.

(b) The correct answer is:

	✓
Mini servers for each employee	
Extra-large hard drives for PCs	
Cloud-based storage	✓
Large capacity memory sticks	

Cloud-based storage has more protection from cyber threats and is away from the employee's home so data will be protected from loss or damage that may occur there (such as theft or fire etc).

(c) Data in mapping charts can be drilled into.

Dashboards and mapping charts can be drilled into.

(d) The correct answer is:

	✓
True	✓
False	

Data regarding data subjects is protected by data protection legislation. Only individuals (not companies) can be a data subject.

(e) The correct answer is:

	✓
Firewall	
Patch management	
Webcam manager	✓
Access control	

Webcam manager is a cyber security threat where the cyber-attacker uses software to take control of the user's webcam. The other options are all methods of cyber security.

(f) The correct answers are:

	✓
Irrecoverable debts expense account	✓
Rent receivable account	
Bank general ledger account	✓
Ordinary share capital account	

The bank account could be positive, or it could be overdrawn. When debts are written off as irrecoverable it will result in a debit balance (expense). However, if those debts are then recovered when they have previously written off this can lead to an overall credit balance on the irrecoverable debts expense account in the year the debts are recovered.

(g) (i) Discounted net value: £ 2,070

Discounted net value = (£2,300 × 90%) = £2,070

(ii) VAT amount: £ 414

Standard rated VAT is (£2,070 × 20%) = £414

(h) The correct answer is:

	✓
£700 increase	
£660 increase	✓
£700 decrease	
£660 decrease	

The allowance is calculated after excluding the irrecoverable debt.

Closing allowance = (£90,000 − £2,000) × 2% = £1,760.

Adjustment (increase) = closing allowance less opening allowance = £1,760 − £1,100 = £660.

Task 3

(a) The correct answers are:

	✓
A bank error meant a direct debit that was recorded in the cash book was paid twice by the bank, but one payment was refunded by the bank the next day.	
A cheque included in the cash book on the last day of the month did not show on the bank statement until the first week of the following month.	
Interest received showing on the bank statement is not included in the cash book.	✓
A BACS receipt from a customer is showing on the bank statement but your colleague couldn't find an entry for this in the cash book.	✓

The cash book should reflect the interest received and the BACs receipt as these are genuine transactions for the period not captured in the cash book.

The cheque has now cleared and the discrepancy was just a timing difference. It was already reflected in the cash book, so no amendment to the cash book is necessary.

The bank error was subsequently resolved and the cash book already reflected the valid direct debit payment, so no cash book adjustment is needed for this.

(b) The correct answers are:

Statement	True ✓	False ✓
If the bank account in the general ledger and the bank statement are in agreement the company financial statements should show a debit balance of £2,108 on the bank account.	✓	

There is a credit balance on the bank account because the bank essentially owes the company back the money it has invested in the bank. From the company's point of view the cash in the bank is an asset so it is shown as a debit balance.

(c) The correct answers are:

Statement	True ✓	False ✓
Contra entries are adjusted in the receivables ledger control account and payables ledger control account but do not affect the subsidiary receivables and payables ledgers.		✓

A contra will reduce both the receivables ledger control account balance and the payables ledger control account balance. A contra will also need to be updated in the subsidiary ledgers to reduce the balances attributable to the individual customer and supplier records.

(d) When you correct this, you should debit the payables ledger control account by £ 1,048 .

Purchases credit notes should have been debited to the payables ledger control account. To correct the error a debit of £1,048 is needed (2 × £524) which will remove the original erroneous entry in the control account and then reflect the correct entry.

(e) When correcting the error made relating to the rent payment, the correcting entry will not result in an entry to the suspense account.

The rent error will not be reflected in the suspense account as it is a reversal of entries error and will still allow the trial balance to balance.

(f) Corrected balance on receivables ledger control account: £ 18,103 .

The receivables ledger control account needs to be adjusted for the credit note and the sales daybook error. The invoice has been posted to the wrong side in the subsidiary ledger but not the control account and therefore no correction to the control account is required.

	£
Draft receivables control account balance	18,225
Credit note not recorded	(2,122)
Undercast sales daybook	2,000
Corrected receivables control account balance	18,103

(g) The Money Laundering Reporting Officer

You should report your suspicions to your firm's Money Laundering Reporting Officer (MLRO).

(h) The correct answer is:

	✓
The police	
The National Audit Office	
The National Crime Agency	✓
The AAT	

Where suspicion is upheld the MLRO must submit a Suspicious Activity Report (SAR) to the National Crime Agency as soon as it is 'reasonably practicable'.

BPP Practice Assessment 2

EPA Knowledge Assessment

Time allowed: 2 hours 30 mins (90 minutes for the assessment and a further 60 minutes for reflection and planning as needed)

EPA Knowledge Assessment
BPP Practice Assessment 2

Assessment information

You have **2 hours and 30 minutes** to complete this practice assessment.

- This assessment contains **3 tasks** and you should attempt to complete every task.
- Each task is independent. You will not need to refer to your answers to previous tasks.
- The total number of marks for this assessment is **40**.
- Read every task carefully to make sure you understand what is required.
- Where the date is relevant, it is given in the task data.
- Both minus signs and brackets can be used to indicate negative numbers unless task instructions state otherwise.
- You must use a full stop to indicate a decimal point. For example, write 100.57 not 100,57 or 10057.
- You may use a comma to indicate a number in the thousands, but you don't have to. For example, 10000 and 10,000 are both acceptable.

Task 1 (20 marks)

You are an Accounts Assistant for Company B. Company B manufacturers electronic components.

You are assisting with the preparation of the financial statements for the year ended 31 March 20X4, including accounting for any necessary year-end adjustments and corrections.

You have been told you may need to apply your management accounting and tax knowledge during your year end work.

Today is 24 April 20X4.

Company B has sold goods totalling £2,500 on credit to an established customer. The goods sold were not subject to VAT. You have discovered that the sale was not entered into the accounting records and you now need to record the sale.

Required

(a) How will the elements of the accounting equation be affected by recording the sale?

	✓
Increase both assets and liabilities by £2,500	
Increase both capital and assets by £2,500	
Decrease both capital and liabilities by £2,500	
Increase capital by £2,500 and decrease liabilities by £2,500	

(1 mark)

You are calculating the depreciation for the year ended 31 March 20X4 on some specialist manufacturing equipment which was purchased on 1 January 20X4. The equipment cost £19,000 and the cost of installing and assembling the machine was £1,000. Company B also paid £500 on the date of acquisition for a year's maintenance of the equipment.

The equipment has a useful life of four years and the residual value at the end of the useful life is expected to be £4,000. Company B calculates depreciation on an annual basis with a full year's depreciation charged in the year of acquisition.

Required

(b) Calculate the depreciation for the year ended 31 March 20X4.

£ [   ] (1 mark)

Company B is considering trying to obtain a loan of £25,000 from the bank in 20X5 to help expand its operations. Repayments are expected to start in 20X7.

Required

(c) If the company is successful in obtaining the bank loan, indicate which two sections of the statement of financial position will be affected by the receipt of the loan.

	✓
Current liabilities	
Current assets	
Non-current assets	
Non-current liabilities	

(2 marks)

You are reviewing the financial results for the period and comparing them to budgeted figures.

Required

(d) Calculate the sales variance and indicate whether it is adverse or favourable.

	Budgeted (£)	Actual (£)	Variance (£)	Adverse/Favourable
Sales	457,635	463,124		▼

Picklist
- Adverse
- Favourable

(2 marks)

(e) Which of the following reasons might explain the sales variance?

	✓
Reduced idle time	
Strict quality control	
Increased selling price per unit	
Increased competition in the market	

(1 mark)

Part of your role is to balance off the control accounts.

Required

(f) Balance off the receivables ledger control account shown below.

	£		£
Sales	340,000	Bank	160,000
▼		▼	
Total		Total	
▼		▼	

Picklist
- Balance b/d
- Balance c/d
- Capital
- Profit and loss account
- Sales

(3 marks)

You have now moved on to looking at the VAT records.

Required

(g) Which of the following would appear on a VAT invoice?

	✓
The date from which the company became VAT registered	
The address and VAT number of the supplier	
The VAT registration number of the purchaser	
The time of supply	

(2 marks)

Company B has the following sales and purchases in the current VAT quarter.

	£
Standard rated sales (VAT-exclusive)	250,000
Zero rated sales	80,000
Standard rated purchases (VAT-inclusive)	65,000
Zero rated purchases	10,000

Required

(h) Calculate the VAT due to HMRC.

VAT due £ ☐ (1 mark)

One of your colleagues has recently started her AAT studies and you are explaining the various stakeholders that your business has to her.

Required

(i) Complete the sentence that follows.

You explain to your colleague that the business' ☐▼ are connected stakeholders and that its ☐▼ are external stakeholders.

Picklist
- Competitors
- Corporate management
- Customers
- Employees

(2 marks)

You are reviewing a trial balance report generated from your accounting software and have found the payables control account balance is lower than the total of the supplier account balances in the memorandum.

Required

(j) **Identify which of the following could be a reason for the difference.**

	✓
A supplier invoice for £989 was entered as £998 in the purchases daybook.	
A purchase invoice was allocated to the wrong supplier	
A payment to a supplier recorded in the general ledger was not recorded in the memorandum	
A supplier invoice has been duplicated in the purchases daybook.	

(1 mark)

(k) **Which of the following errors will result in a suspense account being used to account for an imbalance in the trial balance?**

	✓
Rent receivable was recorded correctly in the bank account and debited to the rent receivable account	
Repairs to equipment were posted to a non-current asset account	
Discounts allowed were not posted to the general ledger	
A sales credit note was allocated to the wrong account in the memorandum	

(1 mark)

You notice that a trade receivables balance treated as an irrecoverable debt last year has recently been paid by the customer.

Required

(l) **Complete the sentence that follows.**

The entries to record the recovered amount will [▼] the irrecoverable debts expense and [▼] the allowance for doubtful receivables.

Picklist
- Decrease
- Have no effect on
- Increase

(2 marks)

You have been advised that, as normal, you should prepare the financial statements on the assumption that Company B will continue in operation for the foreseeable future.

Required

(m) Select the accounting principle you will be following if you adopt this approach.

	✓
Going concern	
Consistency	
Materiality	
Accruals	

(1 mark)

Task 2 (10 marks)

Company B regularly reviews its accounting systems and makes improvements when the technology allows.

In your role as accounts assistant, you are pleased to make use of the technology but are also conscious of the need to carry out your year-end review of the financial statements with the right level of care and diligence. You have been instructed to correct any errors you discover.

Due to technological advances and ongoing changes to legislation, you regularly have to complete compulsory training modules to keep you up to date with the latest regulations on data protection and money laundering.

Required

(a) Which TWO statements regarding cloud accounting software are correct?

	✓
Cloud accounting software can be integrated with other business systems	
Cloud accounting software is updated by the user at a time which is convenient to them	
Cloud accounting software protects user data by backing up data to storage hardware at the user's location	
Cloud accounting software supports hybrid working	

(2 marks)

(b) Complete the following sentence regarding data visualisation.

Data visualisation tools [▼] in real-time.

Picklist
- Automatically update
- Do not automatically update

(1 mark)

Clara works for Company B's marketing department and is responsible for processing and analysing personal customer data.

Required

(c) In terms of the Data Protection Act, which of the following roles would Clara be classified as doing?

	✓
Data controller	
Data processor	
Data subject	
Data analyst	

(1 mark)

(d) Which of the following statements regarding the Data Protection Act is correct?

	✓
All information about a customer can be stored, even if it does not fulfil a particular purpose at the current time	
Information can only be stored about a customer if they are aware of the purpose it was collected for and whilst it is being used to achieve that purpose	
Information about a customer must be deleted after 6 months	
Information about customers should be checked annually for accuracy	

(1 mark)

Whilst analysing payments and receipts in Company B's current accounts, deposit accounts and investment accounts, you notice a particular (low value) sum of money moving between different accounts over a period of a couple of months for no apparent reason.

Required

(e) Which money laundering activity could be happening?

[▼]

Picklist
- Integration
- Layering
- Placement

(1 mark)

(f) What should your next course of action be regarding these suspicious transfers?

	✓
Nothing – the transfers are of low value and you do not wish to bother your manager with them	
Notify your manager – despite their low value, your manager should be notified before taking the matter further	
Notify the AAT's ethical helpline with your concerns	
Contact the Money Laundering Reporting Officer	

(1 mark)

You are looking at the statement of profit or loss report generated by the accounting software and the amount shown on the general expenses account looks a lot higher than you would expect and is significantly higher than the previous year. Your colleague tells you that the new accounting software you are using has controls built into it, so that you don't need to worry about checking everything.

Required

(g) What action should you take?

	✓
Move on with the rest of your work and rely on the accounting software controls	
Create a journal to move some of the general expenses to purchases so it looks more comparable with last year	
Ask your colleague to finish preparing the accounts	
Review the detail of the general expenses entries to see what the reason for the increase is	

(1 mark)

You have extracted an initial trial balance from the accounting software package which shows a trade payables balance of £21,270. Based on the payment terms you state on your invoices and your experience in general, you would normally expect the trade payables balance to be around £40,000.

Required

(h) Which of the following could help to explain the difference between the trade payables balance extracted from the system and the trade payables balance you would expect?

	✓
A significant purchase from Company B's biggest supplier was made just before 31 March 20X4	
The company made BACS payments to a number of key suppliers on 31 March 20X4 to clear outstanding invoices.	
The company decided to delay payments to a number of suppliers to ease cash flow	
Company B managed to negotiate an increase in its credit limit granted by a main supplier in January 20X4	

(1 mark)

During the year your manager has allocated you time and provided training sessions to ensure you have the required technical accounting and tax knowledge to carry out your monthly tasks.

Required

(i) Which fundamental ethical principle will this help you to comply with?

	✓
Integrity	
Objectivity	
Professional competence and due care	
Confidentiality	

(1 mark)

Task 3 (10 marks)

As Accounts Assistant for Company B, you maintain and reconcile the control accounts to supporting records and to the financial statements. You are responsible to making sure the suspense account is cleared by investigating what has caused any balance on the suspense account and making any necessary adjustments.

You also support a relatively new trainee by answering any queries they have on accounting and taxation matters.

The trainee has asked for your help in understanding which are the fundamental qualitative characteristics of useful financial information.

Required

(a) Complete the sentences that follows.

The fundamental qualitative characteristic which is concerned with whether a financial item or situation is complete, neutral and free from material error is [▼] .

Picklist
- Comparability
- Faithful representation
- Relevance
- Timeliness
- Verifiability

(1 mark)

Your trainee asks you about making some corrections. They are reconciling the payables ledger control account to the subsidiary payables ledger.

Required

(b) Identify which TWO of the following items will require an adjustment to the payables ledger control account.

	✓
A payment allocated against the wrong supplier subsidiary account	
The purchases returns total of £1,243 was entered in the general ledger as £1,234	
A cash book total was added up incorrectly and resulted in a low payments total being entered in the payables ledger control account	
A contra entry posted to the general ledger was missed when updating the customer and supplier subsidiary ledgers.	

(2 marks)

The suspense account has a debit balance of £7,620. It has been discovered that £4,420 of the debit balance relates to a single error which has not yet been detected.

The other £3,200 debit balance relates to the payment of a trade payable which was correctly recorded in the bank general ledger but incorrectly recorded as a credit to purchases of £1,600.

Required

(c) (i) Which of the following single errors could have resulted in the £4,420 debit balance in the suspense account?

	✓
A receipt from a customer for £2,210 correctly posted to the receivables control account and credited to sales.	
A receipt from a customer for £2,210 correctly posted to the receivables control account and debited to sales.	
A customer invoice for £4,420 correctly posted to the receivables control account but omitted from the customer account in the subsidiary ledger.	
A payment to a supplier for £4,420 omitted from the cash book and the from the supplier account in the subsidiary ledger.	

(1 mark)

(ii) What entries are needed to correct the error that resulted in the £3,200 debit balance in the suspense account?

	✓
DR Trade payables control account £3,200, CR Suspense £3,200	
DR Suspense £3,200, CR Trade payables control account £1,600, CR Purchases £1,600	
DR Bank £1,600, DR Purchases £1,600, CR Suspense £3,200	
DR Trade payables control account £1,600, DR Purchases £1,600, CR Suspense £3,200	

(1 mark)

160 EPA Knowledge Assessment

At the start of the period, the balances on the control accounts were as follows:

Account	£
Payables ledger control account	20,219 CR
Receivables ledger control account	42,654 DR

During the period:

- Goods were sold to credit customers totalling £94,888
- Purchases were made from suppliers on credit totalling £51,922
- Receipts from credit customers totalled £88,612
- Payments to suppliers totalled £49,331
- Contra entries totalling £2,900 were made

Required

(d) Calculate the balances on each of the control account accounts after the transactions for the period have been entered.

Account	£
Payables ledger control account (CR)	
Receivables ledger control account (DR)	

(2 marks)

Your trainee asks how the credit balance relating to an overdrawn bank account would be presented in the financial statements.

Required

(e) Complete the following statement.

A bank overdraft would be included within [▼] in the financial statements.

Picklist

- Current assets
- Current liabilities
- Equity
- Expenses
- Non-current liabilities

(1 mark)

You have reported a money laundering concern to the appropriate person in your organisation.

Required

(f) (i) Complete the following statement.

That person will need to file a [▼] Report

Picklist

- Criminal Activity
- Money Laundering Activity
- Suspicious Activity

(1 mark)

(ii) **Complete the following statement.**

The report will need to be sent to the [▼] .

Picklist
- Police
- Financial Conduct Authority
- National Crime Agency

(1 mark)

BPP Practice Assessment 2

EPA Knowledge Assessment

Answers

Task 1

(a) The correct answer is:

	✓
Increase both assets and liabilities by £2,500	
Increase both capital and assets by £2,500	✓
Decrease both capital and liabilities by £2,500	
Increase capital by £2,500 and decrease liabilities by £2,500	

The credit sale leads to an increase in assets (a receivable) and in revenue which increases the overall capital. There is no impact on liabilities.

(b) £ 4,000

The asset cost is £20,000 = £19,000 for the equipment + £1,000 for the installation and assembly. The maintenance costs should not be capitalised under IAS 16 Property, Plant and Equipment.

The annual depreciation is (£20,000 – £4,000) / 4 = £4,000.

(c) The correct answers are:

	✓
Current liabilities	
Current assets	✓
Non-current assets	
Non-current liabilities	✓

The loan will initially be recorded as DR bank (current assets), CR bank loan (non-current liabilities).

(d)

	Budgeted (£)	Actual (£)	Variance (£)	Adverse/Favourable
Sales	457,635	463,124	5,489	Favourable

The actual sales figure is more than budget, therefore it is a favourable variance.

(e) The correct answer is:

	✓
Reduced idle time	
Strict quality control	
Increased selling price per unit	✓
Increased competition in the market	

To achieve a favourable sales variance, the business must have either sold products at a higher selling price, increased the volume of units sold or a combination of the two. Increased competition would have the opposite effect, either reducing selling prices or volumes sold.

Idle time affects the labour variance and strict quality control affects the materials variance.

(f)

	£		£
Sales	340,000	Bank	160,000
		Balance c/d	180,000
Total	340,000	Total	340,000
Balance b/d	180,000		

(g) The correct answers are:

	✓
The date from which the company became VAT registered	
The address and VAT number of the supplier	✓
The VAT registration number of the purchaser	
The time of supply	✓

(h) VAT due £ 39,166.67

Output VAT = £250,000 × 20% = £50,000

Input VAT = £65,000 × 1/6 = £10,833.33

VAT due = £50,000 − £10,833.33 = £39,166.67

(i) You explain to your colleague that the business' customers are connected stakeholders and that its competitors are external stakeholders.

Stakeholders can be classified as:

Internal:
- Corporate management (eg directors)
- Employees

Connected:
- Shareholders
- Intermediate (business) and final (consumer) customers
- Suppliers

External:
- Immediate community/society at large
- Competitors
- Special interest groups
- Government

(j) The correct answer is:

	✓
A supplier invoice for £989 was entered as £998 in the purchases daybook.	
A purchase invoice was allocated to the wrong supplier	
A payment to a supplier recorded in the general ledger was not recorded in the memorandum	✓
A supplier invoice has been duplicated in the purchases daybook.	

A supplier invoice entered as £998 instead of £989 would make the general ledger balance higher than the memorandum total.

A purchase invoice allocated to the wrong supplier would not result in a difference in the totals.

The payment in the general ledger (but not to the related supplier account in the memorandum) would decrease the payables control and make it lower than the total of the supplier account balances in the memorandum.

Duplicated invoices in the purchases daybook increase the payables control balance.

(k) The correct answer is:

	✓
Rent receivable was recorded correctly in the bank account and debited to the rent receivable account	✓
Repairs to equipment were posted to a non-current asset account	
Discounts allowed were not posted to the general ledger	
A sales credit note was allocated to the wrong account in the memorandum	

Rent receivable should be credited to the rent receivable account so debiting to bank and rent receivable results in two debit entries for the transaction. This would result in a balance on the suspense account to force the trial balance to balance.

(l) The entries to record the recovered amount will ⌐decrease⌐ the irrecoverable debts expense and ⌐have no effect on⌐ the allowance for doubtful receivables.

The cash received is offset against the irrecoverable debts expense account (it reduces the expense in the statement of profit or loss). The debt is not taken into account in the allowance for doubtful receivables as it was written off previously.

(m) The correct answer is:

	✓
Going concern	✓
Consistency	
Materiality	
Accruals	

Going concern: The financial statements are normally prepared on the assumption that an entity will continue in operation for the foreseeable future.

Task 2

(a) The correct answers are:

	✓
Cloud accounting software can be integrated with other business systems	✓
Cloud accounting software is updated by the user at a time which is convenient to them	
Cloud accounting software protects user data by backing up data to storage hardware at the user's location	
Cloud accounting software supports hybrid working	✓

Cloud accounting improves the integration of software as, for example, customer relationship management software can be linked to accounting software. It allows simultaneous access by multiple users and from multiple locations (which supports flexible and hybrid working). Cloud-based software is usually updated and backed up automatically by the software provider (with the backed-up data stored in the cloud rather than locally).

(b) Data visualisation tools [automatically update] in real-time.

Data visualisation tools update in real-time which means that information is kept up-to-date and is ready to be analysed.

(c) The correct answer is:

	✓
Data controller	
Data processor	✓
Data subject	
Data analyst	

Organisations that process personal data (such as Company B) are known as data controllers. Data processors (such as Clara) are responsible for processing personal data on behalf of a data controller. Data subjects are identified or identifiable individuals (such as Company B's customers). Data analyst might be a job title, but it is not a role identified by the Data Protection Act.

(d) The correct answer is:

	✓
All information about a customer can be stored, even if it does not fulfil a particular purpose at the current time	
Information can only be stored about a customer if they are aware of the purpose it was collected for and whilst it is being used to achieve that purpose	✓
Information about a customer must be deleted after 6 months	
Information about customers should be checked annually for accuracy	

Customers must be notified that their information is being collected and the purpose that it is being collected for. Information should not be kept once the purpose has been achieved. Only information that is needed to achieve the purpose it is collected or can be stored. There is no such rule regarding deleting data after six months or annual accuracy checks (businesses are only required to take reasonable steps to ensure data is not incorrect or misleading).

(e) Layering

The money laundering process usually comprises of three distinct phases:

Placement – the disposal of the proceeds of crime into an apparently legitimate business property or activity.

Layering – the transfer of money from place to place, in order to conceal its criminal origins.

Integration – the culmination of placement and layering, giving the money the appearance of being from a legitimate source.

(f) The correct answer is:

	✓
Nothing – the transfers are of low value and you do not wish to bother your manager with them	
Notify your manager – despite their low value, your manager should be notified before taking the matter further	
Notify the AAT's ethical helpline with your concerns	
Contact the Money Laundering Reporting Officer	✓

If you do nothing, then you may be committing the offence of failure to report money laundering. You should not notify your manager because if money laundering is occurring and they are involved then you may be committing the offence of tipping off. The AAT's ethical help line will help with ethical issues, but this is a legal one and you have a legal duty to report your suspicions. Your next course of action is to contact your Money Laundering Reporting Officer.

(g) The correct answer is:

	✓
Move on with the rest of your work and rely on the accounting software controls	
Create a journal to move some of the general expenses to purchases so it looks more comparable with last year	
Ask your colleague to finish preparing the accounts	
Review the detail of the general expenses entries to see what the reason for the increase is	✓

It is important to exercise professional scepticism when reviewing outputs from accounting software. Any controls built into the system cannot be relied upon here as they are unlikely to make sure expenditure is posted to the correct expense account. The reason for the increase should be investigated by you (as your colleague has indicated they are unlikely to look into this matter) and any errors found should be corrected.

(h) The correct answer is:

	✓
A significant purchase from Company B's biggest supplier was made just before 31 March 20X4	
The company made BACS payments to a number of key suppliers on 31 March 20X4 to clear outstanding invoices.	✓
The company decided to delay payments to a number of suppliers to ease cash flow	
Company B managed to negotiate an increase in its credit limit granted by a main supplier in January 20X4	

The BACS payments on the last day of the month would reduce the closing trade payables balance. All of the other options are likely to result in an increase in payables.

(i) The correct answer is:

	✓
Integrity	
Objectivity	
Professional competence and due care	✓
Confidentiality	

The training will help you to maintain professional knowledge and skill at the level required. This is consistent with the definition of the fundamental principle of 'professional competence and due care' set out in AAT's *Code of Professional Ethics*.

Task 3

(a) The fundamental qualitative characteristic which is concerned with whether a financial item or situation is complete, neutral and free from material error is faithful representation.

Information that provides a faithful representation of a financial item or situation must be complete, neutral and free from material error.

(b) The correct answers are:

	✓
A payment allocated against the wrong supplier subsidiary account	
The purchases returns total of £1,243 was entered in the general ledger as £1,234	✓
A cash book total was added up incorrectly and resulted in a low payments total being entered in the payables ledger control account	✓
A contra entry posted to the general ledger was missed when updating the customer and supplier subsidiary ledgers.	

Where there are errors in daybook totals, this feeds through into the general ledger entries that will later need correcting in the control account.

(c) (i) The correct answer is:

	✓
A receipt from a customer for £2,210 correctly posted to the receivables control account and credited to sales.	✓
A receipt from a customer for £2,210 correctly posted to the receivables control account and debited to sales.	
A customer invoice for £4,420 correctly posted to the receivables control account but omitted from the customer account in the subsidiary ledger.	
A payment to a supplier for £4,420 omitted from the cash book and the from the supplier account in the subsidiary ledger.	

The receipt from the customer credited to sales would have meant credit entries made would have been 2 × £2,210 = £4,420 (CR Receivables control account £2,210, CR Sales £2,210). This would have needed a corresponding debit entry of £4,420 to be made to the suspense account to make the debits and credits on the trial balance equal.

(ii) The correct answer is:

	✓
DR Trade payables control account £3,200, CR Suspense £3,200	
DR Suspense £3,200, CR Trade payables control account £1,600, CR Purchases £1,600	
DR Bank £1,600, DR Purchases £1,600, CR Suspense £3,200	
DR Trade payables control account £1,600, DR Purchases £1,600, CR Suspense £3,200	✓

The original entry should have been DR Trade payables control account £1,600, CR Bank £1,600. The erroneous credit to purchases needs to be reversed by debiting purchases, and the payment of the trade payable needs to be reflected by debiting £1,600 to the trade payables control account. The bank entry was accounted for correctly so does not require amending. The balancing entry is to credit the suspense account by £3,200.

(d)

Account	£
Payables ledger control account (CR)	19,910
Receivables ledger control account (DR)	46,030

The period end balances can be calculated as follows:

	Payables ledger control account (£)	Receivables ledger control account (£)
Balance at the start of the period	20,219	42,654
Sales		94,888
Purchases	51,922	
Receipts		-88,612
Payments	-49,331	
Contras	-2,900	-2,900
Balance at the period end	19,910	46,030

(e) A bank overdraft would be included within current liabilities in the financial statements.

A bank overdraft is a credit balance presented within current liabilities.

(f) (i) That person will need to file a Suspicious Activity Report

The appropriate person (Money Laundering Reporting Officer) needs to file a Suspicious Activity Report.

(ii) The report will need to be sent to the National Crime Agency .

The appropriate person (Money Laundering Reporting Officer) needs to file a Suspicious Activity Report.

BPP Practice Assessment 3

EPA Knowledge Assessment

Time allowed: 2 hours 30 mins (90 minutes for the assessment and a further 60 minutes for reflection and planning as needed)

EPA Knowledge Assessment
BPP Practice Assessment 3

Assessment information

You have **2 hours and 30 minutes** to complete this practice assessment.

- This assessment contains **3 tasks** and you should attempt to complete every task.
- Each task is independent. You will not need to refer to your answers to previous tasks.
- The total number of marks for this assessment is **40**.
- Read every task carefully to make sure you understand what is required.
- Where the date is relevant, it is given in the task data.
- Both minus signs and brackets can be used to indicate negative numbers unless task instructions state otherwise.
- You must use a full stop to indicate a decimal point. For example, write 100.57 not 100,57 or 10057.
- You may use a comma to indicate a number in the thousands, but you don't have to. For example, 10000 and 10,000 are both acceptable.

Task 1 (20 marks)

You are an Accounts Assistant for Company C, which sources and sells a wide range of vehicle parts.

You are helping with year-end processes to finalise the general ledger balances for the year ended 31 March 20X4 and the subsequent preparation of the financial statements. This includes accounting for any necessary year-end adjustments and corrections.

You have been asked some management accounting and tax queries by some colleagues who are assisting you.

Today is 24 April 20X4.

Your manager has stressed the importance to you of the qualitative characteristics of useful financial information.

Required

(a) Select which one of the following requests made by your manager is associated with timeliness?

	✓
You should prepare the final accounts shortly after the company's year-end so that we can make decisions for the upcoming financial year.	
You should post similar expenses to the same accounts each financial year.	
We should be able to agree transactions to supporting documentation.	
You should prepare the accounts on the basis that the company will continue to operate and trade for the foreseeable future.	

(1 mark)

(b) Calculate the liabilities figure using the accounting equation.

	£
Assets	92,698
Liabilities	
Capital	51,244

(1 marks)

You are reviewing the inventory included in the statement of financial position to see if it complies with IFRS Accounting Standards.

Required

(c) Which of the following should be excluded from the cost of inventory under IAS 2 *Inventories*.

	✓
Selling costs	
Delivery costs	
Storage costs of finished goods	
Costs of conversion including direct labour	

(2 marks)

IAS 2 *Inventories* require inventory to be measured at the lower of cost and net realisable value (NRV) on an individual item basis.

Required

(d) **Complete the following sentence**

The net realisable value of inventory is the [▼] .

Picklist

- Expected selling price less completion costs less selling and distribution costs
- Expected selling price less estimated storage costs until date of sale
- Market value
- Replacement cost

(1 mark)

At 31 March 20X3 the accounts of Company C showed accrued rent payable of £2,500. During the year to 31 March 20X4 the business paid rent bills totalling £12,750, including one bill for £3,750 in respect of the quarter ending 30 April 20X4.

Required

(e) **What is the statement of profit or loss charge for the rent expense for the year ended 31 March 20X4?**

£ [   ]

(1 mark)

(f) (i) **Complete the following statement.**

An example of a current asset would be [▼]

Picklist

- Accrued expenses
- Accrued income
- Deferred income
- Prepaid income

(1 mark)

(ii) **Complete the following statement.**

The entry to adjust for closing inventory [▼] cost of sales in the statement of profit or loss.

Picklist

- Decreases
- Has no effect on
- Increases

(1 mark)

You have been asked to prepare a cash budget for sales of a new car part which is being launched on 1st February. It is expected that 500 units will be sold each month at a price of £175. All sales are on credit and 75% of the cash will be received in the month after the sale is made with the balance being received two months after the sale.

Required

(g) Calculate the budgeted cash received for March.

£ ☐ (1 mark)

(h) The manager of a cost centre is responsible for:

☐ ▼

Picklist
- Costs and profits only
- Costs only
- Costs, profits and investments
- Investments only
- Profits only

(1 mark)

(i) Which of the following are examples of revenue income? Select all that apply.

	✓
Sale of trading assets	
Sale of non-current assets	
Interest received on cash held at the bank	
Sale of shares held for investment	

(1 mark)

Company C received an order for some goods from a customer on 12 December 20X3 and on that date the customer paid a deposit of £200.

The goods were supplied by Company C on 15 January the following year (20X4).

Company C issued an invoice on 20 January and the customer paid the balance on 29 January.

Required

(j) Answer the following questions on tax points.

(i) Which ONE is correct for the tax point for the deposit?

	✓
12 December 20X3	
15 January 20X4	
20 January 20X4	
29 January 20X4	

(1 mark)

(ii) Which ONE is correct for the tax point for the balance of the payment?

	✓
12 December 20X3	
15 January 20X4	
20 January 20X4	
29 January 20X4	

(1 mark)

A colleague working on year-end payroll has asked you about reporting payroll related information.

Required

(k) Which of the following is true about a Full Payment Submission (FPS).

	✓
A FPS shows the end of year summary of pay and deductions.	
A FPS shows end of year summary of taxable benefits.	
A FPS is a return showing pay and deductions for each employee on a specific payment date.	
A FPS is filed every month.	

(1 mark)

Company C's policy is to charge a full year's depreciation charge in the year of acquisition and none in the year of disposal.

The following details have been extracted from the non-current asset register as at 1 April 20X3.

	Cost £	Accumulated depreciation £	Carrying amount £
Asset X	120,000	20,000	100,000
Asset Y	85,000	70,000	15,000
Asset Z	45,000	20,000	25,000

Asset Y was disposed of on 1 March 20X4 for proceeds of £20,000.

Depreciation on these assets hasn't been calculated for the year ended 31 March 20X4. The assets should be depreciated on a diminishing balance basis at 25% per annum.

Required

(l) (i) Calculate the depreciation expense relating to the assets for the year ended 31 March 20X4

£ [   ]

(1 mark)

(ii) Complete the following sentence.

The entries relating to the disposal of Asset Y will [▼] by £ [   ]

Picklist
- Decrease cash
- Decrease profit
- Increase liabilities
- Increase profit

(2 marks)

Company C is considering making international transactions.

Required

(m) Which TWO of the following statements are true?

	✓
Goods supplied to overseas customers are referred to as exports and are always zero-rated.	
Goods which are purchased from overseas countries are known as imports.	
Goods supplied to overseas customers are referred to as exports and are always zero-rated, provided the trader obtains evidence of their export.	
When the goods enter the UK, the supplier needs to pay the applicable rate of UK VAT.	

(2 marks)

One of your colleagues from another department has sent you an email and asked if you can please provide year-end financial statements by tomorrow as they need them for a meeting. You know that you don't have time before tomorrow to carry out all your normal checks and reconciliations.

Required

(n) In the first instance, which of the following is the most appropriate course of action?

	✓
Reply to the email asking how important the meeting is and, if it is very important, do what you can to get the financial statements ready for tomorrow.	
Discuss your concerns about the time pressure being applied in the email with your immediate line manager or another senior member of your department.	
Delegate a number of tasks to a less experienced team member so you have a chance to meet the deadline.	
Email the colleague back saying you can make the deadline if they can help you prepare the accounts.	

(1 mark)

Task 2 (10 marks)

You are involved in a project for Company C to review how technology is currently used in the business and how the finance systems should be controlled and maintained.

In your role as accounts assistant, you have also been asked to advise on the benefits of the accounting software used, such as automation of processes, along with managing any risks arising.

Finally, you have been learning about legislation relating to money laundering and data protection and your manager is keen to know what you have found out about the regulations during your training.

As part of a review into Company C's technology and information systems, you have been asked to investigate information requirements at different levels within the organisation.

Required

(a) **Which of the following is a characteristic of information at the operational level of a business?**

	✓
Externally sourced	
Structured	
Long-term focus	
Strategic perspective	

(1 mark)

One option to improve financial information at Company C is to install a new module in the business' accounting software. This module will automatically download transactions from the company's bank account into the bank ledger in the accounting software.

Required

(b) **Which of the following technologies does this module use?**

	✓
Blockchain	
Artificial intelligence	
Process automation	
Cloud computing	

(1 mark)

(c) **Complete the following sentence below.**

[▼] refers to the trustworthiness or accuracy of big data.

Picklist
- Value
- Variety
- Velocity
- Veracity
- Volume

(1 mark)

(d) **The Data Protection Act protects the data of both individuals and companies.**

	✓
True	
False	

(1 mark)

(e) **Which of the following cyber security threats involves the use of Bots to overwhelm an organisation's website with internet traffic?**

	✓
Hacking	
Phishing	
Pharming	
DDoS attacks	

(1 mark)

You are considering which accounting processes can be automated by your accounting software package.

Required

(f) **Which two of the following are true in relation to automation of the accounting process using an accounting software package?**

	✓
It is likely that all journal entries can be posted automatically by the accounting package	
Accounting packages can often be used to extract and report a trial balance based on the general ledger	
Many accounting software packages will include functionality that will automatically calculate depreciation based on the depreciation rates and non-current asset balances	
A reduced level of professional scepticism is required when reviewing information produced by accounting software due to the automation involved	

(2 marks)

A colleague has asked you how long VAT records should be retained for as a VAT registered trader.

Required

(g) **Complete the following sentence using the picklists.**

VAT records should usually be retained for [▼] years.

Picklist
- 20
- 3
- 5
- 6

(1 mark)

Company C has reviewed its last 3 VAT returns and found the following errors:

Quarter	Misstatement
1	Overstated output tax £1,000
2	Understated output tax £3,000
3	Understated input tax £3,700

Required

(h) **Which of the following describes the net error?**

	✓
£1,700 payable by the company	
£1,700 repayable to the company	
£300 payable by the company	
£300 repayable to the company	

(1 mark)

Within receivables there is a balance relating to the sale of goods that has been outstanding for 60 days, which is beyond the agreed 30-day credit period. The customer always needs chasing, but usually pays in the end. However, on this occasion you are uncertain as to whether this amount will be paid.

Required

(i) **Select the appropriate course of action in relation to this receivables balance.**

	✓
Set up an allowance for the doubtful receivable	
Decrease the amount of the sales recorded to reflect the fact that the amount is unlikely to be paid	
Write the debt off now as irrecoverable	
Based on the fact the customer usually pays in the end, just make a note of the issue but do not make any adjustments	

(1 mark)

Task 3 (10 marks)

As you have become more experienced as an Accounts Assistant working for Company C, you have been entrusted to prepare reconciliations of the control accounts to supporting records. This sometimes entails making entries to clear the suspense account and making necessary adjustment to either the control accounts or to subsidiary ledgers.

You also reconcile make sure the bank account balance in the general ledger is reconciled to the bank statements each period, making adjustments where necessary.

You are able to escalate issues you can't resolve to more senior staff and also help to support your less experienced colleagues when queries arise on accounting and taxation matters.

The trial balance shows a receivables ledger control account balance that is higher than the total of the customer account balances in the memorandum accounts.

Required

(a) Identity which TWO of the following could be a reason for the difference.

	✓
A credit note issued to a customer was entered in the general ledger but is not showing in the memorandum account.	
A contra entry has been reflected in the memorandum accounts but no general ledger entries have been made.	
A debt due from a customer has been written off as irrecoverable in the general ledger but the full customer balance is still included in the memorandum account.	
An invoice was issued to a new customer in the last few days of the period and was reflected in receivables ledger control account but the customer account has not yet been set up in the memorandum account.	

(2 marks)

You are looking into why there is a balance of £660 on the suspense account and you discover:

- A payment for stationery of £1,450 was correctly posted to the bank account, however, it was posted to the office expenses account as £1,540.
- A payment to settle a supplier invoice for £750 was only reflected in the bank account in the general ledger.
- Rent payment of £900 was posted as a credit to the rent account and a debit to the bank account.

Required

(b) Using the information provided complete the suspense account and clear the outstanding balance.

Suspense account

Details	£	Details	£
Balance b/d	660	▼	
▼		Balance c/d	0
Total		Total	

Picklist

- Bank
- Office expenses
- Payables control
- Rent

(3 marks)

Bank charges and interest noted for the first time when preparing a reconciliation between the cash book and the bank statements will usually require a cash book adjustment.

Required

(c) Identify whether the preceding statement is true or false.

	✓
True	
False	

(1 mark)

You have been asked about the difference between mark-up and margin.

Required

(d) If sales for the period were £320,000 and the profit margin is 40% of sales, what is the expected costs of sales figure?

£ [   ]

(1 mark)

When investigating errors in the end of year figures, you discover a large purchase invoice was omitted from the accounting records. The goods which were purchased were still in inventories at year end and have been included in the year end inventory count.

Required

(e) Identify what effect the omitted purchase invoice will have on the gross profit for Company C.

This misstatement will [▼] the gross profit.

Picklist

- Decrease
- Increase
- Not affect

(1 mark)

You are concerned about some transactions that have gone through Company C's bank account last month.

Required

(f) **Complete the sentence that follows.**

The final stage of the money laundering process is [_____▼].

Picklist
- Integration
- Layering
- Placement

(1 mark)

(g) Once a Money Laundering Reporting Officer (MLRO) has upheld a suspicious activity which has been reported to them, when should they file a Suspicious Activity Report (SAR) with the National Crime Agency?

	✓
Immediately	
Within 7 days	
Within 28 days	
As soon as is reasonably practicable	

(1 mark)

BPP Practice Assessment 3

EPA Knowledge Assessment

Answers

Task 1

(a) The correct answer is:

	✓
You should prepare the final accounts shortly after the company's year-end so that we can make decisions for the upcoming financial year.	✓
You should post similar expenses to the same accounts each financial year.	
We should be able to agree transactions to supporting documentation.	
You should prepare the accounts on the basis that the company will continue to operate and trade for the foreseeable future.	

Timeliness is an enhancing qualitative characteristic. It relates to making information available to users in time to influence their decisions.

(b)

	£
Assets	92,698
Liabilities	41,454
Capital	51,244

Assets − Capital = Liabilities

£92,698 − £51,244 = £41,454

(c) The correct answers are:

	✓
Selling costs	✓
Delivery costs	
Storage costs of finished goods	✓
Costs of conversion including direct labour	

Under IAS 2, selling costs and storage costs of finished goods cannot be included in the cost of inventory.

(d) The net realisable value of inventory is the expected selling price less completion costs less selling and distribution costs .

Net realisable value (NRV): The expected selling price of the item less any further costs to be incurred such as costs to completion and selling or distribution expenses.

(e) £ 9,000

Rent expense

	£		£
Bank	12,750	Accrued expenses (reversal)	2,500
		Prepaid expenses (1/3 × £3,750)	1,250
		Statement of profit or loss	9,000
	12,750		12,750

(f) (i) An example of a current asset would be accrued income

Accrued income is an amount that is due for the period but has not been received – this must be added to the income account balance and included in the statement of financial position as a form of current asset, called 'accrued income'.

(ii) The entry to adjust for closing inventory decreases cost of sales in the statement of profit or loss.

The entry to adjust for closing inventory is to debit closing inventory in the statement of financial position and credit closing inventory in the statement of profit or loss (cost of sales). The credit included in cost of sales decreases cost of sales and increases profit.

(g) £ 65,625

In March, the business will receive 75% of February sales. It will not receive any cash for January because the product was not sold then.

500 × £175 = £87,500

£87,500 × 75% = £65,625

(h) Costs only

The manager of a cost centre is only responsible for the costs of the centre. The manager of a profit centre is responsible for costs and profits and the manager of an investment centre is responsible for costs, profits and investments.

(i) The correct answers are:

	✓
Sale of trading assets	✓
Sale of non-current assets	
Interest received on cash held at the bank	✓
Sale of shares held for investment	

Revenue income is derived from the sale of trading assets and interest and dividends received from investments held by the business.

Capital income is the proceeds from the sale of non-trading assets (ie proceeds from the sale of non-current assets, including investments).

(j) (i) The correct answer is:

	✓
12 December 20X3	✓
15 January 20X4	
20 January 20X4	
29 January 20X4	

The tax point for a deposit is always the date the deposit is paid, being 12 December.

(ii) The correct answer is:

	✓
12 December 20X3	
15 January 20X4	
20 January 20X4	✓
29 January 20X4	

The tax point for the balance is 20 January.

Basic tax point is the date the goods are supplied – ie 15 January.

Actual tax point – Invoice issued within 14 days on 20 January, so the later date applies – ie 20 January.

Date of payment of balance has no impact.

(k) The correct answer is:

	✓
A FPS shows the end of year summary of pay and deductions.	
A FPS shows end of year summary of taxable benefits.	
A FPS is a return showing pay and deductions for each employee on a specific payment date.	✓
A FPS is filed every month.	

A FPS shows the end of year summary of pay and deductions = Form P60.

A FPS shows end of year summary of taxable benefits = Form P11D.

A FPS is filed every time employees are paid.

(l) (i) £ 31,250

No depreciation is charged on Asset Y in the year of disposal. Depreciation on the other assets is calculated as follows.

	Depreciation £
Asset X (100,000 × 0.25)	25,000
Asset Z (25,000 × 0.25)	6,250
Total	31,250

(ii) The entries relating to the disposal of Asset Y will [increase profit] by £ [5,000]

There is a profit on disposal equal to the proceeds less the carrying amount = 20,000 – 15,000 = £5,000.

(m) The correct answers are:

	✓
Goods supplied to overseas customers are referred to as exports and are always zero-rated.	
Goods which are purchased from overseas countries are known as imports.	✓
Goods supplied to overseas customers are referred to as exports and are always zero-rated, provided the trader obtains evidence of their export.	✓
When the goods enter the UK, the supplier needs to pay the applicable rate of UK VAT.	

Goods supplied to overseas customers are referred to as exports and are always zero-rated, **provided the trader obtains evidence of their export**. If there is no evidence of export the supply cannot be zero rated.

Goods purchased from overseas countries are known as imports.

When the goods enter the UK, **the purchaser** needs to pay the applicable rate of UK VAT.

(n) The correct answer is:

	✓
Reply to the email asking how important the meeting is and, if it is very important, do what you can to get the financial statements ready for tomorrow.	
Discuss your concerns about the time pressure being applied in the email with your immediate line manager or another senior member of your department.	✓
Delegate a number of tasks to a less experienced team member so you have a chance to meet the deadline.	
Email the colleague back saying you can make the deadline if they can help you prepare the accounts.	

At all times accountants must maintain their integrity and professional conduct in the work environment, and not be influenced or pressurised into rushing the preparation of financial information. Only staff qualified and experienced enough to carry out the year end tasks should be involved in completing the year end process so you shouldn't delegate any of these tasks to less experienced staff or staff in other departments.

Task 2

(a) The correct answer is:

	✓
Externally sourced	
Structured	✓
Long-term focus	
Strategic perspective	

Operational-level information is generally:

- Structured, eg sales and inventory reports
- Internally sourced
- Focused on the daily, weekly or monthly operational processes

Strategic-level information is generally:

- Unstructured – no consistent format
- Externally sourced
- Focused on the long-term strategy of the business

(b) The correct answer is:

	✓
Blockchain	
Artificial intelligence	
Process automation	✓
Cloud computing	

Process automation is the ability of systems to perform routine activities (such as downloading bank transactions) without the input of a human.

Artificial intelligence is the ability of a computer system to assist to perform cognitive tasks such as making business decisions, finding patterns in data or helping solve problems.

Blockchain is one form of distributed ledger technology. It is a way of recording transactions in 'blocks' which are linked to one another and secured against being altered using cryptography, based on complex calculations.

Cloud computing is the provision of computing as a consumable service instead of a purchased product. It enables data, system information and software to be accessed by computers remotely as a utility through the internet.

(c) Veracity refers to the trustworthiness or accuracy of big data.

The veracity of big data refers to how trustworthy it is.

(d) The correct answer is:

	✓
True	
False	✓

The Data Protection Act only protects data concerning individuals not companies.

(e) The correct answer is:

	✓
Hacking	
Phishing	
Pharming	
DDoS attacks	✓

In a DDoS (Distributed Denial of Service Attack), the cyber-attacker attempts to disrupt an organisation's online activities by preventing people from accessing the organisation's website. Bots are instructed to overwhelm the organisation's website with a wave of internet traffic so that the system is unable to handle it and may crash.

(f) The correct answers are:

	✓
It is likely that all journal entries can be posted automatically by the accounting package	
Accounting packages can often be used to extract and report a trial balance based on the general ledger	✓
Many accounting software packages will include functionality that will automatically calculate depreciation based on the depreciation rates and non-current asset balances	✓
A reduced level of professional scepticism is required when reviewing information produced by accounting software due to the automation involved	

Automation in accounts packages is most likely for processes that use rules and recurring logic, such as calculation of depreciation, extraction of reports based on the data in the accounting system and recurring transactions.

Not all journal entries can be automated as a number of journals can be for one-off or exceptional events, or correction of errors. These will need expert intervention.

Accountants need to be aware automation bias, where results generated from accounting software packages are generally assumed to be correct because they have less human input which is not necessarily the case. The automation is set up and configured initially with human inputs so is still prone to errors which can be worse sometimes because they will be repeated by the automation until detected.

This means maintaining a **high level of professional scepticism** to ensure that inconsistent results or variations from expectations are questioned when a process is automated in just the same way a manual process is questioned.

(g) VAT records should usually be retained for 6 years.

(h) The correct answer is:

	✓
£1,700 payable by the company	
£1,700 repayable to the company	✓
£300 payable by the company	
£300 repayable to the company	

The net error is £1,700 of input tax repayable.

Quarter	Output tax £	Input tax £	Net £
1	(1,000)		
2	3,000		
3		3,700	
Total	2,000	3,700	1,700

(i) The correct answer is:

	✓
Set up an allowance for the doubtful receivable	✓
Decrease the amount of the sales recorded to reflect the fact that the amount is unlikely to be paid	
Write the debt off now as irrecoverable	
Based on the fact the customer usually pays in the end, just make a note of the issue but do not make any adjustments	

There is doubt over the recoverability of a debt but and therefore a provision should be created. If it was deemed irrecoverable it would be written off but that is not the case here.

Task 3

(a) The correct answers are:

	✓
A credit note issued to a customer was entered in the general ledger but is not showing in the memorandum account.	
A contra entry has been reflected in the memorandum accounts but no general ledger entries have been made.	✓
A debt due from a customer has been written off as irrecoverable in the general ledger but the full customer balance is still included in the memorandum account.	
An invoice was issued to a new customer in the last few days of the period and was reflected in receivables ledger control account but the customer account has not yet been set up in the memorandum account.	✓

A contra entry reflected in the memorandum would have reduced the memorandum total but the lack of a general ledger entry would leave the control account total at the same level.

The invoice posted for the new customer would increase the control total making it higher than the total for the memorandum which doesn't list that customer balance.

The other options would decrease the balance on the control account without impacting the memorandum.

(b)

Suspense account

Details	£	Details	£
Balance b/d	660	Payables control	750
Office expenses	90	Balance c/d	0
Total	750	Total	750

The rent error will not be reflected in the suspense account as it is a reversal of entries error and will still allow the trial balance to balance.

(c) The correct answer is:

	✓
True	✓
False	

Interest and bank charges are often not picked up until the bank statement is reviewed.

(d) £ 192,000

This is calculated as 320,000/100 × 60 = £192,000.

(e) This misstatement will increase the gross profit.

The omission of the purchase means cost of sales will be lower that it would otherwise have been, resulting in an increased gross profit.

(f) The final stage of the money laundering process is integration .

The money laundering process comprises of three distinct phases:

Placement – the disposal of the proceeds of crime into an apparently legitimate business property or activity.

Layering – the transfer of money from place to place, in order to conceal its criminal origins.

Integration – the culmination of placement and layering, giving the money the appearance of being from a legitimate source.

(g) The correct answer is:

	✓
Immediately	
Within 7 days	
Within 28 days	
As soon as is reasonably practicable	✓

Where suspicion is upheld the MLRO must submit a Suspicious Activity Report to the National Crime Agency as soon as it is 'reasonably practicable'.

Tell us what you think

Got comments or feedback on this book? Let us know.
Use your QR code reader:

Or, visit:
https://www.smartsurvey.co.uk/s/GPUBYI/

Need to get in touch with customer service?

www.bpp.com/request-support

Spotted an error?

https://learningmedia.bpp.com/pages/errata